29.96

PEOPLE YOU
SHOULD KNOW

TOP 101 ATHLETES

Edited by Jeanne Nagle

Britannica®
— Educational Publishing —

IN ASSOCIATION WITH

ROSEN
EDUCATIONAL SERVICES

Published in 2014 by Britannica Educational Publishing (a trademark of Encyclopædia Britannica, Inc.) in association with The Rosen Publishing Group, Inc.
29 East 21st Street, New York, NY 10010

Distributed exclusively by Rosen Publishing.
To see additional Britannica Educational Publishing titles, go to rosenpublishing.com

First Edition

Britannica Educational Publishing
J.E. Luebering: Director, Core Reference Group
Anthony L. Green: Editor, Compton's by Britannica

Rosen Publishing
Hope Lourie Killcoyne: Executive Editor
Jeanne Nagle: Editor
Nelson Sá: Art Director
Brian Garvey: Designer, cover design
Cindy Reiman: Photography Manager
Marty Levick: Photo Research

Cataloging-in-Publication Data

Top 101 athletes/editor, Jeanne Nagle.
       pages cm.—(People you should know)
Includes bibliographical references and index.
ISBN 978-1-62275-136-5 (library binding)
1. Athletes--Biography--Juvenile literature. 2. Sports--Biography--Juvenile literature. I. Nagle, Jeanne.
GV697.A1T67 2014
796.092'2--dc23
[B]
                                                                2013033328

Manufactured in the United States of America

On the cover: A panoply of top athletes are pictured, including (top, left to right) Cristiano Ronaldo *Gerard Julien/AFP/Getty Images;* Mia Hamm Charley Gallay/Getty Images; Usain Bolt *thelefty/Shutterstock.com;* Jackie Joyner-Kersee *Stephen Lovekin/Getty Images;* (bottom, left to right) Serena Williams *Matthew Stockman/Getty Images;* Michael Phelps *Fabrice Coffrini/AFP/Getty Images;* Peyton Manning *Getty Images;* and Babe Ruth *Library of Congress Prints and Photographs Division.*

Cover and interior pages (top) © iStockphoto.com/René Mansi

CONTENTS

2

32

40

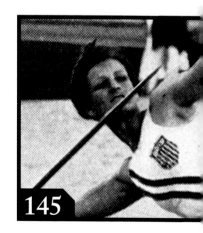

INTRODUCTION

A thletics has been a source of entertainment since the dawn of civilization, from the contests of the ancient Greek Olympics to the various events wherein modern-day, professional athletes of every sport have tested their mettle. Beyond thrilling spectators, however, athletes and the way they have conducted themselves on and off the field of play have also served as an inspiration—and in some cases, a cautionary tale. This book covers both areas of interest, chronicling the personal lives and athletic achievements of some of the greatest sportspersons of all time.

Many of the individuals profiled in these pages are record-holders and record-breakers. Among them is Michael Phelps, who broke Mark Spitz's record for the most medals won by an individual at a single Olympiad. In addition to holding a number of running world records, Usain Bolt is the first person to have won gold medals in two separate events at consecutive Olympiads. Most valuable players (MVPs) and Hall of Famers such as Babe Ruth (baseball), Larry Bird (basketball), Wilma Rudolph (track), Pete Sampras (tennis), and Gayle Sayers (football) are also represented.

Facing adversity, Jim Thorpe was stripped of his amateur status and his Olympic victories lay under a cloud until he was reinstated, unfortunately only after his death. Baseball players Jackie Robinson and Hank Aaron were targets of racial intolerance during their time in major leagues, yet both managed to persevere and excel at their sport. American runner Jesse Owens is famous for upstaging Adolf Hitler's Aryan propaganda by winning four gold medals at the 1936 Berlin Olympics.

Athletes strive to perform well despite setbacks and obstacles. Some obstacles are health-related. Tennis players Andre Agassi and Serena Williams and bicyclist Greg LeMond each overcame possible career-ending—even life-threatening, in the case of Williams and LeMond—injuries and health issues to stage astonishing comebacks in their respective fields. Other roadblocks to glory have been self-inflicted.

Cyclist Lance Armstrong was stripped of all seven of his record-breaking Tour de France titles, and received a lifelong ban from the sport, under the shadow of a blood doping scandal.

A number of athletes have become famous for reasons other than their athletic prowess. Multiple Olympic gold-medal distance runner Emil Zatopek was stripped of his Czechoslovakian military rank, thrown out of the Communist Party, and hindered in his later coaching career after he showed his support for reforms during the Prague Spring of 1968. After she retired from competition, Canadian dual-athlete Carla Hughes became a crusader for mental health patients, committing to perform a cross-country bike ride to raise funds and awareness. Earvin "Magic" Johnson, who was diagnosed with HIV while still an active player, has become a spokesperson in the fight against AIDS since his retirement.

Athletes must possess a strong sense of self, uncommon motivation, and a steely determination to succeed. Each of the profiled athletes have possessed all these traits and more. Learning about the paths they took to the top gives readers a greater appreciation of these athletes' accomplishments, as well as what it means to be an athlete.

HANK AARON

(b. 1934–)

"Throwing a fastball by Henry Aaron is like trying to sneak sunrise past a rooster," St. Louis pitcher Curt Simmons once said, expressing the frustration that pitchers around the league felt while facing one of the most productive power hitters in U.S. major league baseball history. By the start of the 1974 season, Aaron had already rewritten the sport's record book with his brilliant and consistent batting statistics. The best was yet to come, however. On April 8, "Hammerin' Hank" surpassed the mark set by the legendary Babe Ruth with his 715th home run, breaking a record that many experts had long considered untouchable.

Henry Louis Aaron was born on Feb. 5, 1934, in Mobile, Alabama. Even as a young boy, Aaron aspired to play baseball professionally, but he initially played football instead because his high school did not field a baseball team. At age 16 he began playing shortstop with the semi-professional Mobile Black Bears. The next year Aaron was signed for $200 a month by the Indianapolis Clowns, a Negro League team that he had impressed with his performance in an exhibition game. Aaron's raw talent soon caught the attention of scouts from the New York Giants and the Boston Braves, one of whom persuaded the right-handed Aaron to switch his unorthodox, cross-handed batting style to a conventional grip. He hit two home runs in his first game using the new approach.

Aaron spent just a few months with the Clowns in 1952 before the Braves outsmarted the Giants to buy his contract for $10,000. He played shortstop and second base for two seasons on minor league teams in Eau Claire, Wisconsin, and Jacksonville, Florida, winning the Rookie of the Year Award in 1952 and Most Valuable Player (MVP) honors in 1953, before shifting to the outfield while playing in Puerto Rico during the off-season. He joined the Braves, who had moved to Milwaukee, as a starting outfielder for the opening day of the 1954 season after an injury sidelined Bobby Thomson, the expected starter. Aaron posted solid numbers in his rookie year, hitting for an average of .280 with 13 home

Superb batsman Hank Aaron, running the bases during spring training in the 1950s. John Zimmerman/Sports Illustrated/ Getty Images

runs and 69 runs batted in (RBI) despite a broken ankle that limited his season to 122 games. In 1955 Aaron established himself as a perennial all-star with a .314 batting average, 27 home runs, 106 RBI, and 105 runs scored. The following year he won the first of his two National League batting titles with an average of .328 while also leading the league in hits and doubles. Aaron was named the National League's MVP in 1957 after his .322 average and league-leading 44 home runs and 132 RBI helped the Braves capture their first World Series title. In the seven-game championship series, Aaron batted .393 with three home runs against a powerful New York Yankees team.

After the Braves moved to Atlanta in 1966, Aaron continued to post outstanding numbers. In 1970 he recorded his 3,000th hit, becoming only the eighth player to reach the plateau and the first to have both 3,000 hits and more than 500 home runs. A few years later Aaron's pursuit of baseball's most celebrated record—Ruth's all-time home run mark—was accompanied by both intense media pressure and racial intolerance. In 1972 Aaron started receiving hate mail, including death threats, from some baseball fans who were upset to find an African American on the verge of overtaking one of the nation's most beloved sports heroes.

Aaron quietly withstood the pressure with his characteristic cool, but after breaking the record he began using his standing to speak out against the injustices of baseball. A trade sent Aaron back to Milwaukee to play for the American League's Brewers in 1975 and 1976, the final two years of his career.

He retired after 23 seasons with a lifetime batting average of .305 and more career records than any other player in major league history up to that time, including totals of 755 home runs, 2,297 RBI, and 1,477 extra-base hits.

Aaron returned to the Braves in 1976 as vice president in charge of player development. After 13 years in that role, he was appointed a senior vice president and assistant to the team's president. During his tenure in the front office, he remained an often outspoken critic of racial inequality in baseball's administration. He received the Spingarn Medal from the National Association for the Advancement of Colored People in 1975 and was voted into the Baseball Hall of Fame in 1982.

ANDRE AGASSI

(b. 1970–)

At age 18, tennis champion Andre Agassi became the youngest U.S. player to be ranked number one in the world. He first won at Wimbledon in 1992, the U.S. Open in 1994, and the Australian Open in 1995. When he won the French Open in 1999, he became the fifth man in tennis history to win all four Grand Slam events. Bred on the Las Vegas Strip, he was an entertainer on the court, tossing his famous denim shorts and kisses to fans.

Agassi was born on April 29, 1970, in Las Vegas, Nev. By the age of 2, he could serve a tennis ball on a full court, and at age 13 he was sent to a tennis academy in Bradenton, Florida. In 1987 Agassi won his first professional tournament. With six tournament wins in 1988, the right-hander with the powerful forehand began attracting attention.

In 1992 Agassi triumphed at Wimbledon to take his first Grand Slam title. Agassi was then dropped by his coach, who questioned Agassi's dedication to the sport, and he fell out of the top 30 in the rankings. In 1994, he returned with a new coach and a more focused game. Agassi entered the U.S. Open that year as an unseeded player. When he won, it was the first time that an unseeded player had taken the U.S. Open since 1966. In January 1995 he claimed his third Grand Slam title at the Australian Open. He held the number one ranking for 30 consecutive weeks later that year.

A gold medal at the Olympic Games in Atlanta, Georgia, was Agassi's only notable victory in 1996. A recurring wrist injury began to hamper his performances, and his ranking dropped to 141 in 1997. He secured a big comeback in 1999 with wins at the French and U.S. opens and a number one ranking at the end of the year. By the age of 30, he had won more than 40 professional titles and $16 million in prize money. He continued playing in top form, winning the Australian Open again in 2000, 2001, and 2003.

Agassi was married to actress Brooke Shields from 1997 to 1999. In 2001 he married retired German tennis champion Steffi Graf. Agassi himself retired from tennis after competing in the 2006 U.S. Open. His autobiography, *Open*, was published in 2009. In 2011 Agassi was inducted into the International Tennis Hall of Fame.

LANCE ARMSTRONG

(b. 1971–)

Lance Armstrong was the first rider in history to win seven Tour de France titles (1999–2005). All of his titles were later taken away, after an investigation revealed that he was the key figure in a wide-ranging doping conspiracy while he recorded his Tour victories. In addition to losing his titles, Armstrong was banned for life from the sport of cycling.

Armstrong was born in Plano, Texas, on September 18, 1971. He entered sports at a young age, excelling in both swimming and cycling. As a teenager, he competed in triathlons and swimming competitions. Before his high school graduation, the Junior National Cycling Team, part of the U.S. Cycling Federation, had already recruited him. Armstrong competed in Moscow at the Junior World Championships and in 1990 won the U.S.

Amateur Championships. In 1992 he turned professional, joining the Motorola team. One year later he became the second youngest champion in world road racing, and he ranked fifth in world standings. Armstrong won legs of the Tour de France in both 1993 and 1995 but withdrew from three of four Tours he attempted from 1993 to 1996.

After the 1996 Tour de France, Armstrong fell ill, and later that year doctors diagnosed him with testicular cancer, which had by that time also spread to his lungs and brain. He underwent surgery and chemo-therapy. Between treatment sessions, Armstrong still took rides of some 30 miles (48 kilometers). By April 1997 the tumors had disappeared.

In September 1997, Armstrong, unranked and riding with the French Cofidis team, finished a respectable fourth in the Tour of Spain. He joined the United States Postal Service team in October and began preparing for the 1999 Tour de France. He won the opening stage and all three time trials of the 2,254-mile (3,630-kilometer), 22-day race, winning by 7 minutes and 37 seconds. Armstrong was only the second American to win the Tour de France—and the first to win for an American team (three-time winner Greg LeMond had raced with European teams).

During the race, traces of corticosteroid, a banned substance, were found in Armstrong's urine. The International Cycling Union (Union Cycliste Internationale; UCI) cleared him after he produced a prescription for a steroid-based cream used for saddle sores, though the validity of this prescription would later be questioned. Armstrong won the 2000 Tour de France, finishing the 21-stage race 6 minutes and 2 seconds ahead of his nearest competitor. He won the next two Tour de France races with even stronger showings. He finished the 2001 race 6 minutes and 44 seconds ahead of the next cyclist and the 2002 race with a margin of 7 minutes and 17 seconds.

In 2003 Armstrong claimed his fifth consecutive Tour de France, tying a record set by Miguel Indurain of Spain. Armstrong completed the race in 83 hours 41 minutes 12 seconds, beating runner-up Jan Ullrich of Germany by 61 seconds. In 2004 he won his sixth consecutive race with a time of 83 hours 36 minutes 2 seconds, which was 6 minutes and 19 seconds faster than that of the second-place rider, Germany's Andreas Klöden. In 2005 Armstrong extended his sequence of Tour de France wins to seven, finish-ing 4 minutes and 40 seconds ahead of runner-up Ivan Basso of Italy.

Armstrong subsequently retired from the sport, but in 2008 he announced that he was returning to competitive cycling. He placed third in the 2009 Tour de France but slipped to 23rd overall in the 2010 Tour. He retired for a second time in February 2011 and thereafter began competing in triathlons.

In February 2012 a U.S. federal grand jury investigation into doping allegations against Armstrong ended with no criminal charges being filed against him. In June of that year, however, the U.S. Anti-Doping Agency (USADA) alleged that Armstrong and five of his associates had been part of a decade-long doping conspiracy beginning in the late 1990s. According to USADA, Armstrong used performance-enhancing drugs and distributed drugs to other cyclists. The agency also accused him of having undergone blood transfusions and testosterone injections. The allegations resulted in his immediate ban from triathlon competition.

In August 2012 Armstrong declined to enter USADA's arbitration process, which led the agency to announce that it would strip him of all his prizes and awards from August 1998 forward—including his seven Tour de France titles—and pass a lifetime ban from cycling and any other sport that follows the World Anti-Doping Code. Armstrong stated that his decision to no longer contest them was not an admission of guilt but was instead a result of his weariness with having to answer repeated doping questions. The evidence of his doping, however, was so overwhelming that in October 2012 he was officially stripped of his titles and was banned from the sport when the UCI accepted USADA's findings.

In January 2013, during a televised interview with Oprah Winfrey, Armstrong finally admitted to taking performance-enhancing drugs from the mid-1990s through 2005. On the same day that the interview aired, the International Olympic Committee announced its decision to strip Armstrong of the bronze medal he won in the men's road cycling individual time trial event at the 2000 Olympic Games in Sydney, Australia.

Apart from his racing career, Armstrong established the Lance Armstrong Foundation to provide support for cancer patients and to fund cancer research. In the wake of the doping scandal, however, he stepped down as the foundation's chairman, and the charity officially changed its name to the Livestrong Foundation. Armstrong published the memoirs *It's Not About the Bike: My Journey Back to Life* (2000) and *Every Second Counts* (2003), both coauthored by Sally Jenkins.

DAVID BECKHAM

(b. 1975–)

Considered one of the elite players of his sport, David Beckham was perhaps best known for his free kicks and crosses. His shots often appeared to "bend" around players from the other team.

David Robert Joseph Beckham was born on May 2, 1975, in London. At age 11 he won a soccer contest, and one of England's best teams, Manchester United, soon took interest in him. As a teenager, Beckham played for Manchester United's youth squad and led it to a national championship.

In 1995 he began playing with the professional Manchester United team in the Premier League competition, and during the 1995–96 season, he helped the team win the league title and the Football Association (FA) Cup. The following year Manchester United successfully defended its league title, and Beckham was voted Young Player of the Year. In the 1998–99 season Manchester won the league title, the FA Cup, and the European Cup, and Beckham was named the Union of European Football Associations (UEFA) Best Midfielder and the UEFA Club Footballer of the Year. He went on to help Manchester win three more Premier League championships in 2000, 2001 and 2003. The 2002 film *Bend It Like Beckham* paid homage to his kicking ability.

Beckham also played for England's national team for 11 years. He led the team to appearances in the World Cup in 1998, 2002, and 2006. In 2006 he made history by becoming the only player from England's national team to score a goal in three World Cup tournaments. The following year he posted his 100th international appearance, becoming only the fifth person to do so in the history of English soccer.

In 1999 Beckham married singer Victoria Adams, best known as "Posh Spice" of the pop group Spice Girls, in a lavish ceremony. The intense media attention to the couple increased Beckham's popularity around the world, as did his fashionable style of dress and ever-changing hairstyles. In 2003 he was made an Officer of the British Empire (OBE).

After the completion of the 2002–03 season, Beckham left Manchester United. He joined the Spanish soccer club Real Madrid. Four years later he moved to the United States to play for the Los Angeles Galaxy. In October 2008 Beckham signed a deal to play with the Italian team AC Milan during the Galaxy's off-season. In March 2010, while playing for AC Milan, Beckham suffered a tear to his left Achilles tendon that required surgery to repair and knocked him out of competing in his fourth World Cup. Beckham was inducted into the English Football Hall of Fame in 2008.

KENENISA BEKELE

(b. 1982–)

Kenenisa Bekele stands as one of the greatest long-distance runners in history. In addition to winning 11 world cross-country titles, he earned three Olympic gold medals.

Kenenisa Bekele was born on June 13, 1982, near Bekoji, Ethiopia. He attended school through the ninth grade, and it was at school that he was introduced to running. In 1998 he won a provincial cross-country title and placed sixth in the Ethiopian junior championships. His success led to an invitation to join the Mugher Cement Factory team, coached by Tolosa Kotu, then the Ethiopian national marathon coach. In 1999 Bekele placed ninth in the junior race at the world cross-country championships and took the silver medal in the 3,000 meters at the International Association of Athletics Federations (IAAF) world youth championships.

At the 2001 world cross-country championships, Bekele placed second in the senior short-course, a 2.5-mile (4 km) event and won the junior race by a 33-second margin. At the 2002 world cross-country championships he won both the senior long-course and short-course titles—a feat never before accomplished by a male runner. An Achilles tendon injury cut short Bekele's 2002 track season, but in March 2003 he was healthy and competed in the world cross-country championships, where he repeated his astonishing double victory. He would go on to win both races at the world cross-country championships in 2004, 2005, and 2006, setting a record for most career wins in the history of the championships. The short-course race was thereafter eliminated from the world cross-country championships, but in 2008 Beleke captured another world long-course title.

Bekele also had tremendous success on the track. He defeated world-record-holder Haile Gebrselassie in the 10,000 meters at the 2003 IAAF Grand Prix in Hengelo, Netherlands. Later that year he won gold medals at both the IAAF world championships (in the 10,000 meters) and at the IAAF World Athletics Final (in the 3,000 meters).

Ethiopian long-distance runner Kenenisa Bekele, acknowledging the crowd after his gold-medal performance in the 3,000-meter race at the 2009 IAAF World Athletics Finals in Greece. thelefty/Shutterstock.com

At the 2004 Olympic Games in Athens, Greece, Bekele won the silver medal in the 5,000 meters and the gold in the 10,000 meters. He won a second 10,000-meter world championship in 2005, and in 2006 he won gold medals in the 3,000 meters at the IAAF world indoor championships and in the 5,000 meters at the IAAF World Athletics Final. He again won the 10,000-meter world championship in 2007, which he followed with two gold medals (in the 5,000 meters and 10,000 meters) at the 2008 Olympic Games in Beijing, China.

In 2009 he won his fourth consecutive world championship in the 10,000 meters, tying Gebrselassie's record. Additionally, over the course of his long-distance dominance in the early 21st century, Bekele broke the world record in the 5,000-meter and 10,000-meter races a number of times. Although Bekele had hoped to secure a third consecutive Olympic gold in the 10,000 meters at the 2012 Games in London, England, he finished fourth in the event.

LARRY BIRD

(b. 1956–)

Larry Bird transformed the Boston Celtics during the 1980s, and also brought back basketball as a popular sport worldwide. He won the Most Valuable Player (MVP) award three times and led his team to 10 Atlantic Division titles and three National Basketball Association (NBA) championships in his 13-year career.

Larry Joe Bird was born on December 7, 1956, near French Lick, Indiana. In high school his accuracy on the basketball court made him a local celebrity and he was recruited by coach Bobby Knight of Indiana University in 1975. However, homesickness led him to leave after only 3 1/2 weeks at school. A year later, he was recruited to play basketball for Indiana State University, where he became an immediate phenomenon. Bird became one of the highest-scoring individuals in the National Collegiate Athletic Association (NCAA). In his senior year, Bird led the team into the 1978–79 NCAA championship game with a 33–0 season record. The contest between Bird's Indiana State and Magic Johnson's Michigan State foretold the professional rivalry between the two. Indiana State lost the championship game to Michigan State, but Larry Bird defeated Magic Johnson in the vote for college player of the year.

In the summer of 1979, Bird signed a contract with the ailing Boston Celtics. He remained with the Celtics for his entire professional career and sparked one of the greatest single-season turnarounds in NBA history. In 1980, Bird was voted NBA Rookie of the Year. The following year, the revival of the Celtics was complete when Boston won the NBA championship over the Houston Rockets.

At the end of the 1983–84 season, the Celtics faced the L.A. Lakers in the NBA championship series. Boston won the NBA championship, and Bird was voted MVP for the 1983–84 season as well as MVP for the finals.

Larry Bird and Magic Johnson played out one of the greatest rivalries in NBA history. In 1985, the Celtics and the Lakers again advanced to the NBA finals, but the Lakers won. Nevertheless, Bird won his second consecutive season MVP award. The following year, the Celtics won the NBA finals against Houston and Bird also won his second finals MVP award.

Bird's last years on the court were troubled by back problems. He won a gold medal as a member of the 1992 United States Olympic basketball team and retired on August 18, 1992. The Celtics retired his number 33 jersey, and in February 1998 he was elected to the Basketball Hall of Fame.

In 1997, he became head coach of the Indiana Pacers. In his first year, Bird reversed the downward spiral of the Pacers, and they finished the 1997–98 season second only to the Chicago Bulls in the Eastern Conference.

In May 1998, Bird became the fourth rookie coach to win the NBA Coach of the Year award. Bird was only the second player in NBA history, after Tom Heinsohn (also a Celtic) to have earned both the Rookie Player and the Coach of the Year.

CAROL BLAZEJOWSKI

(b. 1956–)

Carol Blazejowski was an American basketball player and sports executive whose playing career featured a number of records and firsts.

Carol Blazejowski was born on September 29, 1956 in Elizabeth, New Jersey. She grew up in Cranford, New Jersey, and began playing basketball on a school team in her senior year of high school in 1974. The following year she joined the team at Montclair (N.J.) State College. A highly competitive player, Blazejowski (known as "Blaze") set long-standing records for the highest women's career scoring average (31.7 points per game [ppg]) and single-season average (38.6 ppg). She was a three-time All-American (1976, 1977, and 1978), and in 1978 she was awarded the first Wade Trophy for Women's Basketball Player of the Year. On March 6, 1977, Blazejowski scored a record 52 points against

11

Queens College before a crowd of 12,000 at Madison Square Garden in New York City.

In 1979 Blazejowski was on the first U.S. women's basketball team to win a gold medal at the World University Games (WUG) in Mexico City. Two years earlier she had played at the WUG in Sofia, Bulgaria, where the U.S. team won a silver medal. Both years Blazejowski was the team's top scorer, with 129 points total (18.4 ppg) in 1979 and 164 points total (20.5 ppg) in 1977. At the 1979 Pan American Games, she was part of the U.S. women's basketball team that won the silver medal.

Although she had been selected for the 1980 Olympic team, Blazejowski was deprived of the opportunity to compete when the U.S. government called a boycott of the Moscow Games. In 1980–81 she played for the New Jersey Gems in the Women's Basketball League (WBL) until the WBL went bankrupt. During that season she led the league in scoring and was named Most Valuable Player. Throughout the 1980s Blazejowski worked in promotions and marketing for sporting-goods firms such as Adidas. In 1990 she took a position with the National Basketball Association (NBA) in the Consumer Products Group.

While working for the NBA, she became involved in the development of the Women's National Basketball Association (WNBA). Before the WNBA's debut in the summer of 1997, she signed on as vice president and general manager of the New York Liberty professional team. She was promoted to president of the team in 2008 but left the Liberty in 2010. In 1994 Blazejowski became one of the few women inducted into the Naismith Memorial Basketball Hall of Fame.

USAIN BOLT

(b. 1986–)

U sain Bolt was born on August 21, 1986, in Montego Bay, Jamaica. Nicknamed "Lightning Bolt," he became the first person to win gold medals in both the 100- and 200-meter races in consecutive Olympiads.

A track prodigy, he won the 200-meter event at the 2002 world junior championships at the age of 15. He also competed in the

Jamaican runner Usain Bolt, taking on the competition during a first-round heat at the 2012 Olympic Games in London. Michael Steele/Getty Images

200-meter event at the 2004 Olympics in Athens, Greece, but was hampered by a hamstring injury and failed to advance beyond the first round of heats.

Though he stood 6 feet 5 inches (1.96 meters), Bolt challenged the common belief that very tall sprinters are disadvantaged as fast starters. In 2007 he earned a silver medal in the 200-meter event at the world championships. After persuading his coach to let him try the 100 meters, he ran 10.03 seconds in his first professional race at the distance. In May 2008 he broke the world record in the 100 meters, running 9.72 seconds.

At the 2008 Olympic Games, Bolt became the first man since American Carl Lewis in 1984 to win the 100 meters, 200 meters, and 4 × 100-meter relay in a single Olympics and the first ever to establish world records (9.69 seconds, 19.30 seconds, and 37.10 seconds, respectively) in all three events. He also won gold medals in all three events at the 2009 world championships while setting new world marks in the 100 meters (9.58 seconds) and 200 meters (19.19 seconds).

Bolt was the heavy favorite in the sprint events heading into the 2011 world championships, but a false start disqualified him from the 100-meter final. He recovered to capture gold medals in the 200 meters and the 4 × 100-meter relay, helping to set a new world record (37.04 seconds) in the latter event.

Although Bolt lost both the 100- and 200-meter races to training partner Yohan Blake at the 2012 Jamaican Olympic Trials, he was back in top form weeks later at the London Olympics, where he set an Olympic record in the 100 meters (9.63 seconds) and claimed another decisive victory in the 200-meter event. Bolt also powered the Jamaican team to a new world record in the 4 × 100-meter relay (36.84 seconds).

TOM BRADY

(b. 1977–)

A s quarterback, Tom Brady led the New England Patriots of the National Football League (NFL) to three Super Bowl victories (2002, 2004, and 2005) and was twice named the game's MVP (2002, 2004).

Thomas Edward Patrick Brady, Jr. was born on August 3, 1977 in San Mateo, California. While growing up, Brady often attended San Francisco 49ers games to watch the legendary quarterback and his idol Joe Montana play. In high school Brady excelled in both football and baseball. He entered the Major League Baseball draft in 1995 and was picked by the Montreal Expos, but he decided instead to attend the University of Michigan and play football. Brady, who did not start until his junior year, led Michigan to victory in the 1999 Orange Bowl and gained a reputation as a determined and intelligent player. In 2000 he was chosen in the sixth round of the NFL draft by New England, and he worked diligently during his first season to improve his strength and technique.

In the second game of the 2001 season, the Patriots' starting quarterback, Drew Bledsoe, was injured, and Brady was chosen to fill the position. The Patriots went on to post an 11–3 record in the regular season and upset the St. Louis Rams in Super Bowl XXXVI. Brady also was named the Super Bowl MVP. The Patriots became one of the NFL's elite teams, posting an incredible 40–12 record during Brady's first three seasons. In 2004 the team returned to the Super Bowl, defeating the Carolina Panthers and earning Brady another Super Bowl MVP award. The momentum carried through to the next season, as the Patriots extended their consecutive win streak to 21, breaking the record of 18 set by the Miami Dolphins in 1972–73. Brady and the Patriots capped off the season with their third Super Bowl in four years, this time against the Philadelphia Eagles.

In the 2007 season Brady threw a record 50 touchdown passes, and he led New England to the first 16–0 regular season in NFL history, earning NFL MVP honors in the process. However, the Patriots lost to the underdog New York Giants in Super Bowl XLII. In the first game of the 2008 NFL schedule, Brady suffered a severe knee injury that required season-ending surgery. He returned to form the next season, earning a Pro Bowl selection after guiding the Patriots to another play-off berth. Brady led the NFL with 36 touchdown passes in 2010 and helped the Patriots to a league-best 14–2 record. Despite the Patriots getting upset in their first play-off game the following postseason, he was named league MVP a second time, becoming the first player to capture the award unanimously. During the 2011 season Brady passed for 5,235 yards to become—along with new record holder Drew Brees—one of two quarterbacks to surpass Dan Marino's record. However the Patriots lost to the Giants again in February 2012.

While not the strongest or the quickest quarterback in the NFL, Brady established himself among the game's greats for his drive, his intelligent playmaking abilities, and the remarkable leadership he provided under pressure. Brady married fashion model Gisele Bündchen in 2009.

JAMES BROWN

(b. 1936–)

The leading football player of his time, Jim Brown led the National Football League (NFL) in rushing yards for eight of his nine seasons. He ranks among the best running backs of all time.

James Nathaniel Brown was born in St. Simons, Georgia, on February 17, 1936. In high school and at Syracuse University in New York, he displayed exceptional all-around athletic ability, excelling in basketball, baseball, track, and lacrosse as well as football. In his final year at Syracuse, Brown earned All-America honors in both football and lacrosse.

Running back James Brown (center, No. 32), breaking a tackle in the 1960s. Focus On Sport/Getty Images

From 1957 through 1965 Brown played for the Cleveland Browns of the NFL, and he led the league in rushing yardage every year except 1962. He ran for more than 1,000 yards in seven seasons and established NFL single-season records by rushing for 1,527 yards in 1958 (12-game schedule) and 1,863 yards in 1963 (14-game schedule), a record broken by O.J. Simpson in 1973. On Nov. 24, 1957, he set an NFL record by rushing for 237 yards in a single game, and he equaled that total on Nov. 19, 1961.

At the close of his career, he had scored 126 touchdowns, had gained a record 12,312 rushing yards, and had a record combined yardage (rushing along with pass receptions) of 14,811 yards. Brown's rushing and combined yardage records stood until 1984, when both were surpassed by Walter Payton of the Chicago Bears.

At 30 years of age and seemingly at the height of his athletic abilities, Brown retired from football to pursue a career in movies. He appeared in many action and adventure films, among them *The Dirty Dozen* (1967) and *100 Rifles* (1969). Brown was also active in issues facing African Americans, forming groups to assist black-owned businesses and to rehabilitate gang members. He was elected to the Pro Football Hall of Fame in 1971.

WILT CHAMBERLAIN

(b. 1936–d. 1999)

W ilt Chamberlain was the first outstanding 7-footer in basketball and is still considered by some as the greatest offensive player in the history of the game. The press nicknamed him "Wilt the Stilt," but he preferred to be called "the Big Dipper."

Wilton Norman Chamberlain was born in Philadelphia on Aug. 21, 1936. When he was a senior in high school, hundreds of colleges offered him basketball scholarships. He chose the University of Kansas, a school with a strong basketball tradition, and was there from 1955 to 1958. He played one season with the Harlem Globetrotters, an exhibition team, and then in 1959 joined the Philadelphia (later, San Francisco) Warriors of the National Basketball Association

(NBA). After only one season with the Warriors, he was named the league's Most Valuable Player. During the 1961–62 season he claimed three NBA records when he scored 4,029 points in 80 regular-season games, reached an average of 50.4 points a game, and scored 100 points in a single game.

In the middle of the 1964–65 season Chamberlain was traded to the Philadelphia 76ers. In 1966 he became the second NBA player to attain a career total of 20,000 points, and the next season he led his team to the NBA title and reached a record 68.3 shooting average. Before the 1968–69 season, Chamberlain was traded to the Los Angeles Lakers because of his high salary demands.

In 1968 he reached a record 25,000 career points and became the first center to lead the league in assists. Chamberlain's powerful presence drove the Lakers to the 1972 NBA title and helped them win a record 33 consecutive victories. When he retired in 1973, he had a record total of 23,924 rebounds and 31,419 points. He was named to the Basketball Hall of Fame in 1978. Chamberlain died on Oct. 12, 1999, in Los Angeles.

TY COBB

(b. 1886–d. 1961)

C onsidered one of the greatest and fiercest players in the history of baseball, Ty Cobb was the first man elected to baseball's Hall of Fame. He was a left-handed batter, but he threw right-handed.

Tyrus Raymond Cobb was born on December 18, 1886, on his grandfather's farm near Narrows, Georgia. His Georgia upbringing was the inspiration behind his baseball nickname, "the Georgia Peach." He became a major-league player as an outfielder with the American League's Detroit Tigers in 1905, a position he held for 22 seasons. He also managed the Tigers from 1921 through 1926 and returned to playing actively from 1927 to 1928 with the Philadelphia Athletics.

At 6 feet 1 inch and 175 pounds—particularly big for a baseball player at the time—he looked frightening to basemen as he slid in with his shoe spikes leading the way. He set a lifetime record of 892 stolen bases, and in 1915 he stole 96 bases in 156 games, a record that lasted until 1962. Cobb was a powerful hitter as well. He set a batting record for runs scored of 2,245 and of runs batted in of 1,937. His record-breaking lifetime batting average of .366 remained unbroken into the 21st century. (Sports statisticians disagree as to the exact figure for Cobb's lifetime batting average and runs-batted-in total.)

For 23 years straight he smashed out batting averages of at least .300, and at age 41, when he played his last season, he hit .323. He led the American League in batting 12 times, nine in a row from 1907 through 1915, and in three seasons he hit over .400 (1911, .420; 1912, .410; and 1922, .401). His lifetime hits totaled 4,189.

Cobb created or equaled more records than any other baseball player. Some of his batting records were not broken until the 1970s. In 1936 he was elected to the Hall of Fame by a record 98 percent of the vote. He died in Atlanta, Georgia, on July 17, 1961.

BOB COUSY

(b. 1928–)

A basketball player and coach, Bob Cousy was generally regarded as the greatest ball-handling guard in basketball history. He was considered a bit short for a professional at 6 feet, 1 inch (1.85 meters). He starred at the College of the Holy Cross before breaking into the National Basketball Association (NBA).

Bob Cousy was born on Aug. 9, 1928, in New York. During his career with the Boston Celtics from 1950 to 1963, he led the NBA in assists for eight consecutive years and compiled a record-setting 937 assists in championship play. His exact and often remarkable blind passing earned him the nickname "Houdini of the Hardwood." He coached the Boston College Eagles from 1963 to 1969 and the NBA's Cincinnati/Kansas City Royals from 1969 to 1974. He was elected to the National Basketball Hall of Fame in 1970. In 1975 he became the first full-time commissioner of the American Soccer League, a post he held until 1979.

JOE DIMAGGIO

(b. 1914–d. 1999)

Joe DiMaggio was one of the greatest hitters and center fielders in major league baseball. He played for the New York Yankees from 1936 to 1942 and from 1946 to 1951, helping them win nine World Series.

Joseph Paul DiMaggio was born on November 25, 1914, in Martinez, California. Known as "the Yankee Clipper," he led the American League (AL) in batting in 1939 and 1940 and set a major-league record in 1941 by hitting safely in 56 consecutive games. He

New York Yankee "Joltin' Joe" DiMaggio, swinging away during a game against the Cleveland Indians in 1936, DiMaggio's rookie season. Transcendental Graphics/Hulton Archive/Getty Images

was chosen as the American League's Most Valuable Player three times—in 1939, 1941, and 1947.

DiMaggio retired with 361 home runs and a lifetime batting average of .325. He was elected to the Baseball Hall of Fame in 1955.

NOVAK DJOKOVIC

(b. 1987–)

Novak Djokovic was one of tennis's premier performers in the early 21st century, when he won five Grand Slam titles.

Djokovic took up tennis at age four and quickly ascended the junior ranks. Despite the hardships that came with growing up in the war-torn Serbia of the 1990s, he became Europe's top-ranked 14-and-under player and later the number one 16-and-under player on the continent before turning professional in 2003. Djokovic entered the top 100 of the Association of Tennis Professionals (ATP) at age 18, and in July 2006 he won his first ATP event. After advancing to the semifinals at both the 2007 French Open and Wimbledon, he reached the finals of that year's U.S. Open but lost in straight sets to Roger Federer. Djokovic's hot play continued into 2008 as he won the first Grand Slam tournament of the year, the Australian Open, becoming the first Serbian man to win one of tennis's four most prestigious singles championships.

Djokovic's progress plateaued for almost three years, as he won just 10 ATP men's singles tournaments and reached only one Grand Slam final (the 2010 U.S. Open) between February 2008 and the end of 2010. His fortunes turned in December 2010 when he led the Serbian Davis Cup team to the country's first Davis Cup title. His Davis Cup victories marked the beginning of a 43-match winning steak—the third longest such streak in the Open era (since 1968)—which included a second Australian Open title in January 2011. Djokovic's remarkable streak ended with a French Open semifinal loss to Federer, but his strong play helped him rise to the number one world ranking shortly after he defeated Rafael Nadal to capture the 2011 Wimbledon championship. Djokovic later defeated Nadal in the U.S. Open final to claim his third Grand Slam title of the year. At the Australian Open in 2012, he again bested Nadal, winning a five-set thriller that lasted nearly six hours. The two met for the fourth consecutive Grand Slam final at the 2012 French Open, where Djokovic lost to Nadal in four sets. In 2013 Djokovic defeated Andy Murray to win his fourth Australian Open title.

ANNE DONOVAN

(b. 1961–)

A productive basketball player on both the collegiate and international levels, Anne Donovan was often credited with revolutionizing the center position in women's basketball. Donovan began her playing days at Old Dominion University with big shoes to fill, immediately following the end of future Hall of Famer Nancy Lieberman's career.

Anne T. Donovan was born on November 1, 1961, in Ridgewood, New Jersey. A 6-foot, 8-inch (2-meter) college freshman, she faced high expectations as she entered ODU, home of one of the nation's most successful women's basketball programs. Donovan did not disappoint, helping the Monarchs to a National Collegiate Athletic Association (NCAA) national championship in her first season. She went on to establish a storied collegiate career (1979–83), capping it with her selection as national player of the year in 1983.

Donovan was a three-time All-American (1981–83). She led the nation in rebounding in 1982, and set school records in scoring (2,719 points), rebounding (1,976), and blocked shots (801). Her total of 801 blocks also set the all-time NCAA record. She was notable in the classroom as well, earning GTE-CoSIDA Academic All-American honors in 1982 and 1983; she was inducted into the GTE-CoSIDA Academic All-American Hall of Fame in 1994.

Donovan also represented the United States at competitions on the international level. She was named to the United States Olympic team three times (1980, 1984, and 1988) and contributed to the gold-medal drives of 1984 and 1988, making her one of only two women basketball players to win two gold medals. Donovan was also selected to play on seven United States national teams between 1977 and 1988 and was a co-captain of world championship and Pan American teams in 1986 and 1987.

Following graduation, Donovan followed various avenues to keep her basketball career active. She played semiprofessionally in Japan from 1983 to 1988 and in Italy from 1988 to 1989. In 1989 she returned to the United States to accept an assistant coaching position at her alma mater. Donovan remained on the Old Dominion staff until 1995, when she became head coach at East Carolina University. Donovan also was a member of the coaching staff of the 1997 United States national team. In addition to coaching, she worked with several other organizations involved with women's basketball, including serving on the executive committee to USA basketball and the organizing committee for the 1996 Summer Olympics in Atlanta, Georgia.

Donovan was widely recognized as the ideal center that altered the profile of the position in women's basketball. While she was a dominant presence around the offensive and defensive basket, she still was mobile enough to run the floor, had good passing skills, and had an above-average shooting range of 15–17 feet. Donovan was widely regarded as the first center to develop into a complete player. She was inducted into the Basketball Hall of Fame in 1995.

LANDON DONOVAN

(b. 1982–)

Landon Donovan, was an American professional football (soccer) player, is widely regarded as the greatest American male player in the history of the sport.

Donovan was born on March 4, 1982 in Ontario, California. A star player in high school Donovan joined the U.S. national under-17 (U-17) team in 1998. His success in U-17 play drew the attention of German club Bayer Leverkusen, which signed the teenage Donovan in 1999. He played on the Bayer reserve team for one season and was called up to the first team in 2000, but he did not appear in a game before being loaned to the San Jose (California) Earthquakes of Major League Soccer (MLS) in March 2001.

Donovan was an immediate success in his return to the United States, leading the Earthquakes to an MLS Cup title in his first year

U.S. soccer star Landon Donovan (in white), *working his way past defenders during a 2011 game between the Los Angeles Galaxy and the Philadelphia Union, in Pennsylvania.* Drew Hallowell/Getty Images

with the team. The Earthquakes won a second MLS Cup title in 2003, with Donovan earning U.S. Soccer Athlete of the Year honors as well. He won the award a second time in 2004. In early 2005 he returned to Bayer Leverkusen for two and half months before being acquired by the Los Angeles Galaxy of MLS. He then led the Galaxy to an MLS Cup championship in his first season in Los Angeles, giving Donovan his third league title in five years.

In 2008 he was loaned to the German powerhouse team Bayern Munich for the MLS off-season, playing mostly as a substitute. After guiding the Galaxy to an appearance in the 2009 MLS Cup final (a loss to Real Salt Lake [Utah]), Donovan won the league's Most Valuable Player award and was named U.S. Soccer Athlete of the Year a record-tying third time. In 2010 he made his biggest splash to date as a player on loan when he became one of the featured players with Everton during a short stay in the English Premier League, and the following year he scored the championship-clinching goal to secure another MLS Cup title for the Galaxy. Donovan won his fifth career MLS title in 2012, when he scored the game-winning penalty kick in the MLS Cup final.

While arguably the biggest star in the MLS during his domestic career, Donovan also made his lasting mark on the sport at the international level. In addition to his exploits as a member of the U.S. U-17 team—which included winning the Golden Ball award as Most Valuable Player of the 1999 Fédération Internationale de Football Association (FIFA) U-17 World Championship—Donovan starred on the American under-20 and under-23 teams and played for his country in the 2000 Olympic Games in Sydney. He made his debut with the senior national squad in 2000, scoring a goal in his first match.

Donovan led the United States to a surprising run to the quarterfinals at the 2002 World Cup, but the team failed to replicate its success at the 2006 World Cup, recording just two goals (one of them an opposition own goal) en route to an opening round-robin group stage elimination. In 2008 Donovan became the all-time leading goal scorer in U.S. national team history. He was also a member of three Confederation of North, Central American and Caribbean Association Football (CONCACAF) Gold Cup-winning teams (2002, 2005, and 2007).

JULIUS ERVING

(b. 1950–)

Better known as Dr. J, Julius Erving's amazing airborne moves made him one of basketball's all-time top scorers. He once said of his unique ability: "It's easy once you learn how to fly."

Julius Winfield Erving was born on Feb. 22, 1950, in Hempstead, New York. He started playing basketball in local parks and with a nearby Salvation Army team. In his first year at the University of Massachusetts, he broke records for scoring and rebounding. He left the university in

1971 after his junior year to sign a contract as a forward with the Virginia Squires of the American Basketball Association (ABA).

At 6 feet 6 inches tall, Erving changed the idea of the way the game should be played. His great skill and remarkably large hands worked together to make his ball handling an art. His airborne feats popularized the slam dunk, the hanging rebound, and the finger roll. His ability to block shots and rebound, as well as pass and skillfully handle the ball, encouraged faster and flashier play.

In 1973 Erving moved to the New York Nets and, with an average of 27.4 points and 10.7 rebounds per game, led them to the ABA title. Sports enthusiasts believe that when the NBA (National Basketball Association) absorbed the ABA in 1976, it was primarily to get Erving, who joined the Philadelphia 76ers. His first years in Philadelphia were frustrating because the 76er style of play and tendinitis in his knees limited him. But by the 1979–80 season conditions had changed, and Erving was averaging 26.9 points a game.

Erving's honors included ABA Most Valuable Player in 1974, 1975, and 1976, NBA Most Valuable Player in 1981, and many elections to ABA and NBA all-star teams. He was praised for his team spirit, his work for charities, and his success in business. Before his retirement after the 1986–87 season, Erving became only the third player to score 30,000 points in a professional career.

SAMUEL ETO'O

(b. 1981–)

Samuel Eto'o is a Cameroonian professional football (soccer) player who is considered to be one of the greatest African footballers of all time.

Samuel Eto'o Fils was born on March 10, 1981, in Nkon, Cameroon. He attended the Kadji Sports Academy in Douala, Cameroon, and first came to national recognition while playing for UCB Douala, a second-division club, in the 1996 Cup of Cameroon. At only 16 years of age, he caught the attention of Real Madrid, one of the top teams in Europe. They signed him in 1997, though Eto'o saw little playing time. Eto'o still didn't see much action after joining Cameroon when it qualified for the 1998 World Cup but faltered in the first round.

Eto'o made his name playing for Cameroon during the 2000 African Cup of Nations, where he scored four times, including a crucial goal in the Indomitable Lions' gold-medal victory over Nigeria. His impressive play continued at the 2000 Olympic Games in Sydney, where Cameroon defeated Spain for the first Olympic gold in its history. In the Olympic final, with the Indomitable Lions facing a 2–0 deficit in the second half, Eto'o and teammate Patrick Mboma led the comeback with two goals, forcing extra time. After Eto'o's apparent goal in the final seconds of extra time was called back owing to an offside penalty, the game went into penalty kicks, in which Cameroon prevailed.

Eto'o was lent out to a number of teams by Real Madrid until 2000, when he signed with Real Mallorca of the Spanish League. Eto'o's $6.3 million contract was the largest amount paid by the club at the time. Internationally, he guided Cameroon to a second African Cup of Nations title and a World Cup berth in 2002. While Eto'o was an impressive player for Mallorca, he became the club's all-time leading goal scorer, his team was still considered below the top tier of European football, and he was lured to the powerhouse club FC Barcelona in 2004.

Eto'o continued his stellar play in Barcelona. He won his record third consecutive African Player of the Year award in 2005, and Barcelona won Spanish first-division championships in 2005 and 2006, as well as the Champions League in 2006. In 2008 he became the all-time leading scorer in African Cup of Nations history. Eto'o led Barcelona to a historic season in 2009, when the club captured its first "treble" by winning the national first-division title, Spain's major domestic cup (Copa del Ray), and the continental championship (Champions League). At the end of the season, Eto'o was transferred to Inter Milan. He helped Inter win the 2010 Champions League title, and he was the club's leading scorer with 37 goals during the 2010–11 football seasons. In 2011 Eto'o was transferred to the Russian team Anzhi Makhachkala, receiving what was reported to be one of the richest contracts in football history in the process.

JANET EVANS

(b. 1971–)

Janet Evans was born on Aug. 28, 1971 in Placentia, California. As a 7th grader she wrote in her journal that she wanted to break the world record for swimming 1,500 meters. A few years later she achieved that goal, becoming the first woman to swim 1,500 meters in less than 16 minutes. She also broke the records for 400 and 800 meters and won four Olympic gold medals, more than any previous female American swimmer.

Evans joined a local swim team at the age of 4 and began racing at 5. Before her 16th birthday she set world records in 800- and 1,500-meter freestyle events. Four individual victories in the 1987 United States championships brought her national fame. For the next eight years she never lost a freestyle 800-meter or 1,500-meter race.

At the 1988 Olympics in Seoul, South Korea, Evans' small build—5 feet 5½ inches (166.5 centimeters), 102 pounds (46 kilograms) contrasted with the competition, especially the champion swimmers from East Germany. Nevertheless, Evans won three gold medals, starting with the 400-meter individual medley. She set an Olympic record for the 800-meter freestyle, and she swam the 400-meter freestyle in 4 minutes 3.85 seconds, breaking her own world record.

Her Olympic victories, her youth, and her ready laughter made Evans a media darling in the United States. In 1989 she won seven national championships, received the Sullivan Award as top American amateur athlete of the year, and enrolled as a freshman at Stanford University. After two years of academic and athletic success, she left Stanford when the National Collegiate Athletic Association limited swim practice to 20 hours per week. Supporting herself by commercial product endorsements, Evans moved to Austin, Texas, to swim full time.

At the 1992 Olympics in Barcelona, Spain, Evans became the first woman ever to win a second consecutive gold medal in the 800-meter freestyle. She also took the silver medal in the 400-meter freestyle. After the Olympics she continued to collect national and world titles while completing a communications degree at the University of Southern California.

As Evans approached her third Olympics in 1996 in Atlanta, she did not swim as fast as she had in earlier years, but she made the team and participated in the 400- and 800-meter freestyle races. She was also selected to carry the Olympic torch at the opening ceremony. Evans failed to qualify for the finals in the 400-meter freestyle, and she ended her brilliant swimming career after placing sixth in the finals of the 800-meter freestyle.

CHRIS EVERT

(b. 1954–)

C hristine Marie Evert was born on December 21, 1954, in Fort Lauderdale, Florida. Her father, a tennis instructor, began to teach her the game when she was about 6 years old, and from the age of 10 she was always the champion in her amateur age group.

She entered the limelight in 1970 when she beat the top-ranked player, Margaret Court, in a minor event. When 15-year-old "Chrissie" (her nickname then) beat the 28-year-old reigning champion, she set the style for dozens of teenaged gifted players to follow. In 1971, at the age of 16, she became the youngest player to reach the semifinals of

Chris Evert, on the court at the French Open in 1986. Evert won the women's title in Paris that year, becoming the only seven-time French Open women's title winner. Hulton Archive/Getty Images

the United States Open. By 1972, before she turned professional, she had already been forced to turn down more than $50,000 in prize money.

Composed and nearly flawless on a clay court, Chris Evert had a mental toughness that brought new intensity to women's tennis. In 1976 she became the first million-dollar woman player.

Evert was the first woman since Alice Marble in the 1930s to be ranked number 1 for five consecutive years (1974–78). She again held the top ranking in 1980 and 1981. She won 157 singles titles (18 of them in Grand Slam events), setting a record for both men and women professionals. Her 1986 French Open win marked the 13th consecutive year in which she won at least one Grand Slam singles title. She won the U.S. Open six times (1975–78, 1980, and 1982) and Wimbledon three times (1974, 1976, and 1981).

Between 1973 and 1979 Evert won a record 125 consecutive clay-court matches. Her accomplishments included winning the women's singles title in the United States Clay Court Championships from 1972 through 1975 and in 1979 and 1980. She won the French Open on clay in 1974, 1975, 1979, 1980, 1983, 1985, and 1986—the only seven-time winner of the women's championship.

Evert was engaged to Jimmy Connors in the mid-1970s, when both were ranked at the top of the game. From 1979 to 1987 she was married to the English tennis professional John Lloyd. She married Andy Mill, an American skier and television commentator, in 1988. In late 1989, after she had retired from the tennis circuit, she won five matches to bring another Federation Cup to the United States

BRETT FAVRE

(b. 1969–)

Known for his agility, competitiveness, and field presence, Brett Favre broke all the major National Football League (NFL) career passing records as quarterback of the Green Bay Packers. He was also remarkably durable, setting the record for most consecutive starts by an NFL quarterback.

Brett Lorenzo Favre was born on Oct. 10, 1969, in Gulfport, Mississippi. He grew up in Kiln, Mississippi, and attended the University of Southern

Mississippi, where he became the football team's starting quarterback while a freshman. He was drafted by the NFL's Atlanta Falcons in 1991 but was traded to Green Bay the following year. Originally a backup quarterback, he started for an injured teammate in the third game of the 1992 season and never gave up the position. Favre was named the league's Most Valuable Player (MVP) a record three consecutive times (1995, 1996, and 1997) and led the league in touchdown passes in each MVP year.

At the end of the 1996 season, Favre led the Packers to victory over the New England Patriots in Super Bowl XXXI. He returned to the Super Bowl a year later, but the Packers lost. The team was less successful in the following years, but Favre continued to be productive. He led the league in pass completions in 1998 and 2005, and he had the most passing yards and touchdown passes in 1998 and 2003, respectively. In the 2007 season Favre broke John Elway's record of 148 career wins as a starting quarterback and Dan Marino's all-time records of 420 touchdown passes and 61,371 passing yards. Favre announced his retirement at the end of the 2007 NFL season.

In mid-2008 Favre let it be known that he wanted to return to the NFL, and he was reinstated by the league. The Packers traded him to the New York Jets. Though he was named to his 10th career Pro Bowl in 2008, Favre's one season with the Jets was a disappointment. He led the league in interceptions, and the Jets missed the play-offs. Favre retired for the second time in early 2009. Later that year, however, he again returned to the league and joined the Minnesota Vikings.

Favre had one of his best seasons in 2009 where he set a career high in completion percentage and threw only seven interceptions. He guided the Vikings to a 12–4 record and the National Conference championship game, where they lost to the New Orleans Saints.

ROGER FEDERER

(b. 1981–)

Roger Federer's total of 17 career men's singles Grand Slam championships is the most in tennis history. He also set records for consecutive grass-court victories (65) and consecutive weeks with a number one world ranking (237).

Tennis great Roger Federer playing in the fourth round of the 2012 Australia Open in Melbourne. Neale Cousland/Shutterstock.com

Roger Federer was born on August 8, 1981, in Basel, Switzerland. He played tennis from the age of eight, was the Swiss junior champion at 14, and won the Wimbledon junior singles title in 1998 before turning professional. In 1999 he became the youngest player (at 18 years 4 months) to end the year among the world's top 100, finishing that season at number 64. In 2001 he earned a victory over Pete Sampras to reach the quarterfinals of Wimbledon, and by the end of 2002 he was ranked number six in the world.

In 2003 Federer won his first Grand Slam tournament, at Wimbledon. The following year he successfully defended his Wimbledon title, in addition to winning both the Australian Open and U.S. Open, and concluded the season as the world's top-ranked player. In 2005 Federer won 11 of 15 tournaments, including Wimbledon and the U.S. Open. From July 2003 to November 2005 he also won a modern-record 24 straight tournament finals.

Exhibiting a graceful style and brilliant shot-making abilities, Federer continued to rack up impressive victories over the next several years. In both 2006 and 2007 he captured the Australian Open, Wimbledon, and U.S. Open championships. With his thrilling five-set triumph over rival Rafael Nadal of Spain in the 2007 Wimbledon final, Federer became only the second male player (after Bjorn Borg) in more than 100 years to win five consecutive Wimbledon titles.

In 2008 Federer's 65-match grass-court winning streak came to an end when he lost to Nadal in the Wimbledon final. Federer's unmatched 237 weeks on top of the world tennis rankings also ended that year, as Nadal took the number one spot in August. The following month, however, Federer made history again when he earned his fifth consecutive U.S. Open title, a men's record in the open era. The victory followed Federer's performance at the Olympic Games in Beijing, where he teamed with Switzerland's Stanislas Wawrinka to win the men's doubles gold medal.

In June 2009 Federer won the French Open, thereby completing a career Grand Slam of the four major tennis tournaments. Additionally, the win was his 14th Grand Slam championship, which tied him with Sampras for the most Grand Slam titles among male players.

Federer went on to collect his sixth Wimbledon title that year by defeating American Andy Roddick in a marathon five-set final, and in January 2010 he clinched his fourth Australian Open with a victory over Andy Murray of Great Britain. Federer again defeated Murray in July 2012 to win his record-tying seventh career Wimbledon title. A month later the two men faced off in the gold medal match at the Olympic Games in London, England. This time, however, Federer lost to Murray and had to settle for a silver medal.

WALT FRAZIER

(b. 1945–)

K nown for his flamboyant lifestyle as well as for his talent on the court, Walt Frazier was considered one of the premier guards in the history of the National Basketball Association (NBA).

Walter Frazier was born on March 25, 1945, in Atlanta, Georgia. One of eight children, he experienced racial segregation firsthand during his youth. Even though he was an extraordinary basketball player, he was unable to enroll at either Georgia Tech University or the University of Georgia. Frazier took his talents north, leaving his home state for Southern Illinois University (SIU).

Frazier had quick hands and used firm defense to check opponents. He developed a reputation as a player who delivered under pressure. Frazier was named to the National Collegiate Athletic Association (NCAA) Division II All-American team in 1964 and 1965, his first two years at Southern Illinois. The school later moved up to Division I status in athletics, and in 1967 Frazier was selected Division I All-America and was named Most Valuable Player (MVP) of the National Invitational Tournament (NIT) after leading SIU to the championship. Later that year, the New York Knicks selected Frazier as their fifth pick in the first round of the NBA draft.

Frazier's strong style of play quickly made him a favorite of the team's fans and helped him earn NBA All-Rookie honors in his first season with the Knicks. He was nicknamed "Clyde" because his colorful fashion sense, liking for luxury cars, and calm behavior reminded teammates of the Clyde Barrow character in the film *Bonnie and Clyde*. Frazier was a powerful scorer, though he was neither very fast nor a great leaper. This was because he had a fine shooting touch and was an expert at using smooth moves to get to the basket.

Frazier spent ten seasons with the Knicks, helping his team win NBA championships in 1970 and 1973. From 1967 to 1977, in 759 games with New York, he averaged 19.3 points, 6.3 assists, and 6.1 rebounds per game. Frazier led the Knicks in scoring five times and in assists every year he spent with the team. He was named seven times each to the NBA's All-Defensive first team (1969–75) and the NBA All-Star team (1970–76) and selected MVP of the 1975 All-Star game. After spending the final three years of his career with the Cleveland Cavaliers, Frazier retired in 1980 with 15,581 career points (18.9 points per game), 5,040 assists (6.1 per game), and 4,868 rebounds (5.9 per game) in 825 total games. In 93 career playoff games, he averaged 20.7 points, 3.1 assists, and 6.4 rebounds per game.

Frazier moved almost immediately from the court to the broadcasting booth, starting out as a part-time television analyst for both the Atlanta Hawks and the WTBS network in 1981. Beginning in 1987, the Madison Square Garden Network employed Frazier as the radio analyst for the New York Knicks. He also hosted pre-game and halftime shows for Knicks television broadcasts. Frazier was seen as an innovative broadcaster for including rhyming phrases into his commentary; he was often found consulting his pocket dictionary in an effort to expand his already impressive vocabulary.

Frazier retired as one of the most popular athletes in New York sports history. The Knicks retired his jersey number in 1979, and he was inducted into the Madison Square Garden Hall of Fame in 1984. In 1997 he was honored as one of the NBA's 50 greatest players of all time. Aside from sports, Frazier placed a great emphasis on community involvement and spearheaded a program in which he visited schools to impress upon children the importance of education. He was inducted into the Basketball Hall of Fame in 1987.

LOU GEHRIG

(b. 1903–d. 1941)

Nicknamed "the Iron Horse" by sportswriters, Lou Gehrig played in 2,130 consecutive games on the New York Yankees' regular schedule—a record that stood until 1995 (when it was broken by Cal Ripken, Jr.).

Henry Louis Gehrig was born in New York City on June 19, 1903. On June 1, 1925, Gehrig came into the New York Yankee lineup as a rookie pinch hitter. He hit a single and started one of the most remarkable records in baseball. From that day Gehrig played in every Yankee game, regular and exhibition, until 1939.

His father, an ironworker, spurred young Gehrig's interest in athletics by taking him to a gymnasium. Just before Gehrig graduated from grammar school, his father became too ill to work. Gehrig and his mother worked to support the family, but he still found time for athletics at the High School of Commerce and played on several school teams. At first Gehrig was awkward and uncoordinated, but he practiced constantly to overcome his weaknesses. Even when he became a star Gehrig was the first man on and last man off the practice field.

At Columbia University Gehrig pitched and played outfield and first base. In June 1923 he signed a Yankee contract and was farmed out to Hartford, Connecticut, in the Eastern League for two seasons. Gehrig won the regular first-base position with the Yankees the day following his pinch-hitting assignment. He then played continuously until April 30, 1939.

He had a lifetime batting average of .340 and was twice voted the most valuable American League player. Gehrig hit 493 home runs—49 of them in 1934 and in 1936. He was one of the few men in baseball history to hit four home runs in one game. In 1939 he was elected to baseball's Hall of Fame.

Gehrig then contracted Amyotrophic Lateral Sclerosis or ALS (often called Lou Gehrig's disease), a rare disease causing spinal paralysis, and was forced to retire. He died in Riverdale, New York, on June 2, 1941.

STEVEN GERRARD

(b. 1980–)

Steven Gerrard is an English professional football (soccer) player who was considered one of the most complete footballers in the world in the early 2000s.

Steven Gerrard was born on May 30, 1980, in Whiston, England. Gerrard was discovered by his local upper-division football club, Liverpool FC, at age nine. He played for Liverpool's youth squad and signed a professional contract with them at age 17. His first-team debut came in 1998, and he became a regular contributor the following year. Gerrard had established himself as a star midfielder by the 2000–01 season, when Liverpool won the league, Football Association (FA), and Union of European Football Associations (UEFA) cups, and he earned England's Young Player of the Year honors.

Gerrard was named Liverpool's captain in 2003, at just age 23. In the 2004–05 season he led Liverpool to the club's first Champions League title in 21 years, scoring a key goal in Liverpool's dramatic three-goal comeback against AC Milan in the final. During the following off-season he became involved in a high-profile contract dispute with Liverpool that nearly resulted in his transfer to Chelsea FC before he ultimately re-signed with his longtime club. Gerrard then helped Liverpool win both the 2005–06 FA Cup and UEFA Super Cup, and he was named the Professional Footballers' Association Player of the Year at season's end.

In 2007 Liverpool advanced to the Champions League final for the second time in three years but lost to AC Milan by a score of 2–1. Gerrard scored a career-high 24 goals in the 2008–09 Premier League season, which netted him the Football Writers' Association Footballer of the Year award.

Gerrard was a member of the English national under-21 team, and he debuted with the senior national team in 2000. He made one appearance in the 2000 European Championship (Euro 2000), but an injury kept him out of the 2002 World Cup. Gerrard was a regular contributor to England's runs to the quarterfinals in both the Euro 2004 and the 2006 World Cup. Gerrard was made a Member of the British Empire (MBE) in 2006.

STEFFI GRAF

(b. 1969–)

Steffi Graf dominated tennis in the late 1980s and the 1990s. In 1988 she became the first player since 1970 to win the Grand Slam of tennis—the Australian Open, French Open, U.S. Open, and Wimbledon titles in a single year.

Stephanie Maria Graf was born in Brühl, West Germany (now Germany), on June 14, 1969. Her father coached her at tennis from age 4. At 13 years, 4 months, she became the second youngest player to receive an international ranking. In 1987 she won her first Grand Slam event, defeating Martina Navratilova at the French Open.

Known for her speed, footwork, and powerful forehand, Graf took over the top spot in women's tennis in August 1987 and held it until March 1991, for a record 186 weeks. At age 22 years, 3 months, she became the youngest woman to have won 500 matches.

Her singles victories included four Australian Open titles (1988–90, 1994), six French Open titles (1987–88, 1993, 1995–96, 1999), seven Wimbledon titles (1988–89, 1991–93, 1995–96), and five U.S. Open titles (1988–89, 1993, 1995–96). In Seoul, South Korea, in 1988, she won the first Olympic gold medal given in tennis since 1924.

Soon after losing in the finals at Wimbledon in 1999, Graf, who had been plagued by injuries, retired from the sport. She was inducted into the International Tennis Hall of Fame in 2004.

WAYNE GRETZKY

(b. 1961–)

Wayne Gretzky, left-shooting center for the Edmonton Oilers and the Los Angeles Kings hockey teams, was already on his way to being the Great Gretzky when he was barely 10. He scored three goals within 45 seconds of junior league play. Gretzky was elected MVP for eight consecutive seasons (1979–87) with Edmonton and then, after he was traded to Los Angeles in 1988, took a ninth. Following a brief stint with the St. Louis Blues, Gretzky spent the last three years of his career with the New York Rangers.

Wayne Gretzky was born on January 26, 1961, in Brantford, Ontario. He was just a kid when he began skating in the backyard. Early in his career, when he always faced much bigger kids, Gretzky marked out his favorite position—behind the opponents' net, where he could improvise shots and avoid attacker tactics. Also called the Kid, Gretzky was only 5 when he made an all-star team of 10- and 11-year olds. When he joined the World Hockey Association at 17, he was the youngest player ever in professional ice hockey and became rookie of the year. The next season the Oilers were merged into the National Hockey League (NHL), and Gretzky—deceptively skinny

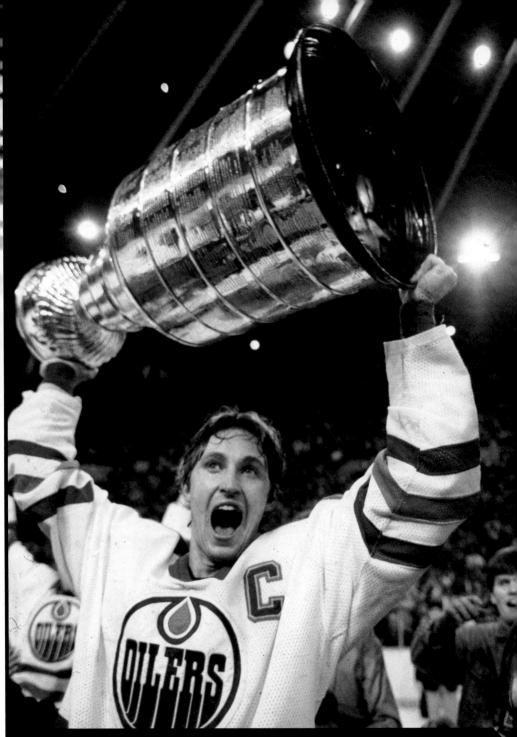

Wayne Gretzky, nicknamed "the Great One," hoisting ice hockey's ultimate trophy, the Stanley Cup, in 1984. Bruce Bennett/Getty Images

and slow, but sensitive on ice—was the NHL's youngest ever Hart Trophy winner for Most Valuable Player (MVP).

Gretzky rewrote the NHL record book. He set all-time season records for assists and points in 1980–81, earning the first of his scoring titles. He kept shattering all the major single-season scoring marks—points (215), goals (92), and assists (163). He established another NHL mark by scoring in 51 consecutive games. In playoffs he was the all-time point leader, and his score of 47 in 1985 set another record. In two of the four years in which he led the Oilers to Stanley Cup titles (1984, 1985, 1987, and 1988) he was voted MVP of the tournament.

In 1989, in only his 780th game and playing against his former team, he broke Gordie Howe's 1,767-game career record of 1,850 points. In 1990 he became the first to score 2,000 points. Gretzky retired on April 18, 1999, bringing an end to one of the most dominant careers in team sports history. At the time of his retirement, Gretzky owned more than 60 NHL records, including records for career goals, assists, and total points.

Soccer's Mia Hamm (right), *playing as part of the United States Women's National Team in a 1999 match against Brazil, in Orlando, Florida.* Tony Ranze/AFP/Getty Images

MIA HAMM

(b. 1972–)

By any measure, the playing career of American soccer (association football) superstar Mia Hamm was astonishing. The Fédération

Internationale de Football Association (FIFA) twice named her the Women's World Player of the Year (2001–02). A powerful striker, she scored more international goals (158) than any other player—male or female—in the history of the sport. Aside from her knack for goal-scoring, Hamm was revered for her all-around skill and competitive spirit.

Mia Hamm was born on March 17, 1972, in Selma, Alabama. At the age of 15 she became the youngest player ever to join the U.S. women's national team, and at 19 she was the youngest member of the U.S. squad that won the World Cup in China in 1991. She was a star of the U.S. team that captured the gold medal at the 1996 Olympics in Atlanta. In 1999 she scored her 108th international goal, breaking the all-time record.

During the 1999 World Cup, Hamm led the U.S. team against China in the legendary final game of that tournament. The game had finished scoreless, and the two nations faced off in a penalty shoot-out. Hamm made one of the penalty shots that set up her teammate Brandi Chastain to score the game-winning penalty kick, and the U.S. national team lifted its second World Cup trophy.

Hamm announced that she would retire after the 2004 Olympics in Athens. She scored twice during the tournament and took the team to the final against Brazil. The United States won the game 2–1, and Hamm left soccer with a new gold medal on her chest. In December 2004, after having played 275 games with the U.S. national team, she hung up her boots for good. In Hamm's first year of eligibility, she was voted into the U.S. National Soccer Hall of Fame in 2007.

FRANCO HARRIS

(b. 1950–)

Franco Harris was an American football running back who was a member of four Super Bowl–winning teams (1975, 1976, 1979, and 1980) as a Pittsburgh Steeler. He is best known for having taken part in arguably the most famous play in National Football League (NFL) history, "the Immaculate Reception."

Franco Harris was born on March 7, 1950 in Fort Dix, New Jersey. He was a star in baseball, basketball, and football during high school, and he earned a football scholarship to Pennsylvania State University (Penn State) in 1968. At Penn State he was often overshadowed by fellow running back Lydell Mitchell, an All-American, but Steelers scouts still saw enough in Harris's play to draft him with the 13th overall selection of the 1972 NFL draft. Having rushed for 1,055 yards and scored 10 touchdowns in his first year in the league, he was named Offensive Rookie of the Year and chosen for the first of nine consecutive Pro Bowls.

The Steelers qualified for the play-offs for the first time in 25 years that season, and their first-round game against the Oakland Raiders was highlighted by Harris's game-winning shoestring catch that came to be known as the Immaculate Reception. The play occurred with 22 seconds remaining in the game and the Steelers trailing 7–6. On fourth-and-10 from the Steelers' 40-yard line, Pittsburgh's quarter-back, Terry Bradshaw, threw a pass that was bent toward the ground by a Raider defender before Harris appeared seemingly out of nowhere to snatch the ball and run into the end zone. Some people believed that the ball either hit the ground before Harris caught it or it was deflected by another Pittsburgh player instead of the Oakland defender, which was illegal at the time; it was ruled a touchdown though, and the Steelers ultimately won the game.

In addition to his Pro Bowl streak, Harris helped the Steelers to eight straight play-off berths from 1972, four of which resulted in Super Bowl titles. He was named Most Valuable Player of Super Bowl IX (1975) after rushing for 158 yards against a tough Minnesota Vikings defense. At 6 feet 2 inches (1.88 meters) and 230 pounds (104 kg), he was a large running back, but he was often criticized for being "soft" because of his tendency to avoid contact that he deemed unnecessary by running out of bounds. However, his cau-tious running style led to a long career: he played 12 seasons with the Steelers and one more with the Seattle Seahawks. At the time of his retirement in 1984, he had the third highest career rushing yardage total in NFL history. Harris was inducted into the Pro Football Hall of Fame in 1990.

THIERRY HENRY

(b. 1977–)

Thierry Daniel Henry was born on August 17, 1977, in Châtillon, France. He is a French football (soccer) player who scored more international goals than any other player in France's history and who is considered one of the most productive goal scorers of his time.

Henry, of French West Indian ancestry, spent his childhood in low-income housing in Les Ulis, south of Paris. He joined FC Versailles in 1992, and, after attracting other club scouts, he was signed by AS Monaco in 1995. Although Henry played as a striker until he was 17, he switched to left wing for Monaco. Monaco won the 1997 French club championship, and Henry's game noticeably improved. Midway through the 1998–99 season, a contract mix-up almost sent him to Real Madrid. Instead, he was transferred to Juventus in Turin, Italy, for £9 million. Seven months later he was on the move again in a £10.5-million deal to join English powerhouse Arsenal.

Arsenal manager Arsène Wenger shifted Henry to striker, giving him more responsibility at the cutting edge of the attack, and the Frenchman soon revealed his true ability. With a deceivingly casual approach, Henry glided past opposing players, initiated and finished moves, and scored goals either with a light touch from short range or fiercely from long distances. In eight seasons with Arsenal he scored a club-record 174 goals, and the team won two league titles (2002, 2004) and two Football Association Cup trophies (2002, 2003).

In mid-2004 Henry won the 2003–04 Golden Shoe as Europe's leading association football goal scorer (with 30) and helped Arsenal to another Premier League championship.

Henry was honored as European Footballer of the Year for 2002 and 2003 and finished runner-up as Fédération Internationale de Football Association (FIFA) World Player of the Year in 2003 and 2004. In 2006 Arsenal advanced to the Champions League final. Although they lost to FC Barcelona, it was the best Champions League finish in the history of the club.

43

In 2007 Henry was transferred to Barcelona for a £16 million fee. There he was a key member of the 2009 team that captured Barcelona's first "treble" by winning the national first-division title, Spain's major domestic cup (Copa del Ray), and the continental championship (Champions League). His play fell off the next year, and he was released by Barcelona in 2010. Henry then signed with the New York Red Bulls of Major League Soccer (MLS). In January 2012 he rejoined Arsenal for a two-month loan during the MLS off-season.

Henry's international honors while playing for France were equally impressive. In 1996 he was a member of the European under-18 championship team, and two years later he played on the French national team that won the FIFA World Cup. In 2000 France added a European championship, and in 2003 Henry had a triple success when he scored the winning goal for France in the FIFA Confederations Cup and was awarded both the Golden Ball (as top player of the tournament) and the Golden Shoe (as top scorer). First selected to play for his country in 1997, Henry scored his 42nd goal in 2007 to become his country's all-time leading scorer in international competition.

GORDIE HOWE

(b. 1928–)

Gordie Howe was a Canadian-born American professional ice hockey player and administrator. His career record of 1,850 total points (goals and assists) in the National Hockey League (NHL) stood until it was broken by Wayne Gretzky in 1989. His record of 801 goals in the NHL was broken by Gretzky in 1994. For three decades Howe entertained fans with his skill and competitive fire and became known for the "Gordie Howe hat-trick," which comprised a goal, an assist, and a fight in a single game.

Gordon Howe was born on March 31, 1928, in Floral, Saskawatch, in Canada. He played hockey from the age of five. In 1944, he moved to the United States and was put on the Detroit Red Wings' negotiating list that same year. He was signed to a contract for Omaha in 1945 and played a season there before joining the Red Wings in 1946. He won the Hart Trophy for the Most Valuable Player of the season several times and was named Canada's Athlete of the Year in 1963.

Howe left the Red Wings in 1971 to play for and become the vice president (president from 1973) of the Houston Aeros in the World Hockey Association (WHA). He played for them with two of his sons through 1977, five seasons after his induction into the Hockey Hall of Fame. He played from 1978 to 1980 with the New England (later the Hartford) Whalers of the WHA, later merged into the NHL.

During his 33-season career, he had 1,071 goals (801 in the NHL) and 1,518 assists (1,049 in the NHL) and played in 2,421 games. After his retirement as a player, Howe became director of player development for the Whalers and chairman of the board for a marketing company.

CLARA HUGHES

(b. 1972–)

A speed skater and cyclist, Clara Hughes has the unique distinction of being one of only five people in the world to have won a gold medal at both the Summer and Winter Olympics. She also rewrote history by winning two medals at the 1996 Atlanta games, becoming the first Canadian woman to ever win a medal in cycling. Hughes also became the second Canadian to ever win a medal in cycling, after Steve Bauer, who won a silver medal at the 1984 games.

Clara Hughes was born on September 27, 1972, in Winnipeg, Canada. As an adolescent, Hughes led a life fuelled by alcohol, drug abuse and constant partying. Being an athlete was the farthest thing from her mind. Hughes then happened to see a televised performance of Gaetan Boucher skating at the 1984 Winter Olympics. She was deeply inspired and that completely turned around her lifestyle. She stopped drinking and taking drugs. She took up speed skating at the age of 16 with a vengeance. However, she switched to cycling just a year later and perfected herself at the sport, training for both road cycling and track cycling. She would only make a return to speed skating a full 12 years later, post her

45

spectacular success at the 1996 Atlanta Olympic Games. Hughes competed in the 3,000- and 5,000-meter speed skating events in the 2006 winter Olympics in Italy, winning gold medals in both events.

As for her cycling, Hughes was the winner of a record eight Pan American gold medals. She participated in the women's Tour de France four times and also took part in three Commonwealth Games, winning gold in one of them. Her crowning glory however, came in the form of the 1996 Summer Olympics.

After her 2006 Olympic win at Turin, Italy, Hughes famously donated $100,000 to Right to Play. She followed Joey Cheek's footsteps, but donated her own earnings, as Canada at the time did not give out bonuses to winning players. After the 2006 Winter Games, Hughes tied with compatriot Cindy Klassen for the most medals won in both Olympics by a Canadian.

Hughes was also the flag bearer of her country at the 2010 Winter Olympics held in Vancouver, Canada. She won a bronze in the 5,000-meter event. In 2012, she announced her cycling comeback in time for the 2012 Summer Olympics in London. Hughes finished in 32nd place and was placed 5th in the individual time trial.

In 2006, she received the Order of Manitoba. In 2007, she was granted the title of an Officer of the Order of Canada. She also became the recipient of an honorary doctorate from the University of Manitoba.

Hughes was inducted into the Canadian Sports Hall of Fame in 2010. She remains a frontrunner for the Right to Play organization, as well as a key spokesperson for the Let's Talk mental health initiative. Hughes recently began a cross country ride across Canada in 2013 to highlight the issue of mental health as well as raise funds for mental health patients. She plans to make the ride an annual event to keep the issue of mental health in the spotlight.

MIGUEL INDURAIN

(b. 1964–)

Miguel Indurain was born on July 16, 1964, in Villava, Spain, near Pamplona, one of five children of Basque farmers. His 1992 victories in the Tour of Italy and the Tour de France made Indurain only the sixth cyclist to win both races in the same year, and he won them both by enormous margins. He defeated the runner-up in Italy by 5 minutes 14 seconds on July 26.

Indurain missed a chance at becoming cycling's third triple-crown winner when he finished sixth in the world road-race championship in his native Spain, but he was in the lead pack of 17 racers at the finish. Even so, with the Spanish road racing championship and victory in Spain's Tour of Catalonia, Indurain was his sport's top-ranked athlete in points and the recipient of *Velo News* magazine's international Cyclist of the Year award.

In the Tour of Italy, he led from the third stage through the end to become its first Spanish winner. In the Tour de France, his second consecutive victory was the fastest in the race's 79 years, as he averaged 24.5 miles per hour (39.5 kilometers per hour) over 2,475 miles (3,983 km) in 23 days.

Indurain was always known for his relaxed, smooth pedaling style. He won his fourth and fifth consecutive Tour de France time-trial stages, always his strength, where cyclists race against the clock with no one benefiting from a competitor's slipstream. His 30.48 miles per hour (49.046 km per hour) speed over 40.4 miles (65 km) in the ninth stage beat the field by 3 minutes. Then his 32.53 miles per hour (52.35 km per hour) speed in the later 39.8-mile (64-km) time trial was the race's best ever in a time trial of more than 31.7 miles (50 km).

He started racing at age 11, when his cousins persuaded him to compete in a nearby race and he finished second. He won his next race, and cycling displaced running and soccer (association football) to become his best sport. After winning several races a year at lower competition levels, he won the Spanish amateur road race championship in 1983 and competed in the 1984 Los Angeles Olympic Games before turning professional in 1985.

In 1989 he won a mountain stage of the Tour de France and finished 17th overall. The next year he finished tenth and likely would have been in the top three if he had not sacrificed himself as a support rider for Banes to team leader Pedro Delgado.

LeBron James

(b. 1984–)

After entering the National Basketball Association (NBA) directly from high school in 2003, LeBron James quickly established himself as one of the league's superstars. An extraordinarily versatile small forward who is capable of playing multiple positions, James was selected as the NBA's Most Valuable Player (MVP) in 2009, 2010, 2012, and 2013, and became only the 10th player in NBA history to have earned that honor in consecutive seasons.

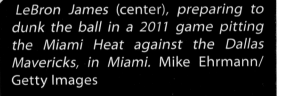

LeBron James (center), *preparing to dunk the ball in a 2011 game pitting the Miami Heat against the Dallas Mavericks, in Miami.* Mike Ehrmann/ Getty Images

LeBron Raymone James was born on December 30, 1984, in Akron, Ohio. In high school, he was named Ohio's Mr. Basketball three times and became a national media sensation in his junior year when he was featured on the cover of *Sports Illustrated*. In his senior season, he was the consensus national high school player of the year before being chosen by the Cleveland Cavaliers as the first overall pick of the 2003 NBA draft.

James made an immediate impact on the Cavaliers, leading the team in scoring, steals, and minutes played during the 2003–04 season on his way to claiming the NBA's Rookie of the Year award. He was named to the NBA All-Star team for the first time in 2005, and in 2007 he guided Cleveland to the franchise's first berth in the NBA finals. Although James posted a remarkable average of 25 points, 8 rebounds, and 8 assists per game throughout the play-offs that year, the Cavaliers were swept in the finals by the San Antonio Spurs.

During the 2007–08 season, James led the NBA in scoring with an average of 30 points per game and became the youngest player in league history to tally 10,000 career points. The following season he led the Cavaliers to a team-record 66 regular-season wins. During both the 2008–09 and 2009–10 seasons, James continued to display his scoring ability, averaging 28.4 and 29.7 points per game, respectively.

At the end of the 2009–10 season James became perhaps the most sought-after free agent in NBA history when his contract with the Cavaliers expired and he began a lengthy courtship process with a number of teams. In a unique hour-long television special on the ESPN sports cable network, James announced that he was going to sign with the Miami Heat.

He helped Miami reach the NBA finals in his first year with the team, but the Heat lost the championship to the Dallas Mavericks. In the 2011–12 season James averaged 27.1 points per game and won his third MVP award while leading Miami to its second consecutive NBA finals appearance. Backed by his brilliant play—James was named the finals MVP—the Heat defeated the Oklahoma City Thunder to win the championship.

In the 2012–13 season James averaged 26.8 points and 8 rebounds per game, earned his fourth MVP award, and led the Heat to another NBA championship. His team defeated the San Antonio Spurs by four games to three in the finals, and James was named finals MVP for the second time.

In addition to his achievements in the NBA, James was a member of the U.S. men's Olympic basketball teams that won the bronze medal at the 2004 Games and the gold medal at both the 2008 and 2012 Games.

DEREK JETER

(b. 1974–)

Derek Sanderson Jeter was born in Pequannock, New Jersey, on June 26, 1974. After an impressive high school baseball record, he was drafted by the New York Yankees as a first-round pick in 1992. He spent a few years improving his skills in the minor leagues before becoming the starting shortstop for the Yankees in 1996.

New York Yankees shortstop and team captain Derek Jeter, exhibiting his fielding skills in an American League Championship game against the Boston Red Sox in 2004. Al Bello/Getty Images

In his first season Jeter posted a batting average of .314 and had 78 runs batted in. He was named AL Rookie of the Year, and the Yankees won the World Series. Jeter continued to play a vital role in the Yankees' success as the team won the World Series in 1998, 1999, 2000, and 2009. With his consistent and timely hitting, Jeter built a reputation as one of the premier postseason hitters in baseball. In 2000 he was named Most Valuable Player of the All-Star Game and the World Series.

From 2004 to 2006 Jeter won three consecutive AL Gold Glove awards as the best-fielding shortstop in the league. In 2009 he recorded his 2,674th career hit, breaking the record for the most hits by a shortstop in major league history. At the end of that season Jeter and the Yankees again won the World Series. On July 9, 2011, Jeter registered his 3,000th career hit, becoming just the 28th player to reach that mark.

MAGIC JOHNSON

(b. 1959–)

The sports world was stunned on November 7, 1991, when Magic Johnson announced his immediate retirement from professional basketball because he was infected with HIV, the virus that causes AIDS (acquired immunodeficiency syndrome). The athlete who, according to one characterization, could "take only three shots and still dominate a game" was slam-dunking a message to defeat HIV ignorance.

Earvin Johnson, Jr., was born in Lansing, Michigan, on August 14, 1959, the sixth of ten children. He got his start playing basketball on the playgrounds of Lansing. As a senior he led the Everett High School team to the Michigan Class A championship. After a particularly amazing display of basketball skill, during which he scored 36 points, grabbed 18 rebounds, and had 16 assists, a Lansing sportswriter christened him "Magic."

Johnson enrolled in his hometown Michigan State University in 1977. His talents led the Spartans to the 1979 NCAA championship during his sophomore year, after which he decided to turn professional.

The 6-foot, 9-inch point guard was drafted by the Los Angeles Lakers in 1979. In his 12 years with the Lakers, the team won five NBA championships (1980, 1982, 1985, 1987, and 1988). He was chosen play-off MVP three times (1980, 1982, and 1987) and was the first rookie to be so named. He was the league's MVP three times (1987, 1989, and 1990), and he was chosen for the 1992 Olympic basketball team. His 9,921 career assists were the most in NBA history.

With his dazzling smile, style, and blind passes, Johnson was among those credited with increasing the popularity of professional basketball in the 1980s. As one of the greatest and most popular players in the history of the NBA, he promised to use his public prominence as a spokesman in the fight against AIDS. He counseled young people to abstain from sex or practice safe sex and warned that contracting HIV "can happen to anybody, even Magic Johnson."

MICHAEL JOHNSON

(b. 1967–)

The first male runner of the 20th century to rank first in the world in both the 200-meter and 400-meter events, Michael Johnson redefined modern track through his mastery of the combined long sprint. He was the first sprinter ever to run the 200-meter in less than 20 seconds and the 400-meter in less than 44 seconds.

Michael Duane Johnson was born on Sept. 13, 1967, in Dallas, Texas, the youngest of five children and the only athlete in his family. He took up track in high school but did not emerge as a serious contender until he was recruited for the relay team by coach Clyde Hart at Baylor University, who eventually became Johnson's trainer. His outstanding early performance was spoiled by repeated hamstring injuries, but under Hart's training he launched the long series of wins in the 200 and 400 meters that made him famous. He earned his first 200-meter gold at the 1990 Goodwill Games, the same year in which he received a bachelor's degree in marketing from Baylor.

Johnson was well known for his unusual running style—back straight, head up, stride short—and for his simple, businesslike approach. At the 1994 Goodwill Games, Johnson won gold medals in the 400 meters and the 4 × 400 relay, and he swept the 1995 World Championships in Göteborg, Sweden, with gold medals in the 200 meters, the 400 meters, and the 4 × 400-meter relay.

His Olympic career was stalled by a broken bone in his leg before the 1988 Olympics in Seoul, South Korea. Sidelined again by food poisoning at the 1992 games in Barcelona, Spain, Johnson still won a team gold medal in the 4 × 400 relay.

Johnson set two world records in the 400-meter indoor sprint in 1995. His top standing in the 200 and 400 meters prompted the International Amateur Athletic Federation to separate the two events so he could compete in both in the 1996 Olympics in Atlanta, Georgia. At the Atlanta Olympics, a hamstring injury kept Johnson out of the 4 × 400 relay, but in a dazzling performance, he became the first man ever to win Olympic gold medals in both the 400 meters and the 200 meters—with a new world record of 19.32 seconds.

Johnson's achievements included 55 consecutive victories in the 400 meters, as well as his gold-medal performance in Atlanta in 1996. The magazine *Track & Field News* named him athlete of the year four times in both the 200-meter and the 400-meter sprint (1990, 1991, 1994, and 1995), and Johnson won the Jesse Owens Award twice (1994 and 1996). The United States Olympic Committee honored him as sportsman of the year in 1993 and again in 1995.

At the 2000 Games in Sydney, Australia, Johnson became the first male Olympian to defend his title in the 400 meters; he did not run in the 200-meter race after failing to qualify at the U.S. trials because of an injury. He also earned a gold medal as the anchor of the 4 × 400-meter relay team. At the Games' conclusion, Johnson announced his retirement from Olympic and world championship competition.

RANDY JOHNSON

(b. 1963–)

With a blazing fastball and a 6-foot, 10-inch (2-meter) frame, Randy Johnson quickly built a reputation as the most feared pitcher in major leaguebaseball. He won five career Cy Young Awards as the best pitcher in either the American or National League.

Randall David Johnson was born on Sept. 10, 1963, in Walnut Creek, California. He earned a scholarship to the University of Southern California, where he played basketball for a few years and starred on the baseball team from 1983 to 1985. He made his major league debut in 1988 with the National League (NL) Montreal Expos.

Johnson was named to the first of his 10 All-Star games in 1990 as a member of the American League (AL) Seattle Mariners. Johnson led the AL in strikeouts for four consecutive years (1992–95), and in 1995 he won the AL Cy Young Award.

After the 1998 season Johnson signed with the NL Arizona Diamondbacks. He led the NL in earned run average, innings pitched, and strikeouts on his way to the 1999 NL Cy Young Award. Johnson won Cy Youngs in each of the following three seasons. His most impressive feat, however, took place at the 2001 World Series, where he tied a record with three wins in a single World Series while guiding the Diamondbacks to their first championship. Johnson and fellow pitcher Curt Schilling shared Most Valuable Player honors for the series.

After pitching for two seasons with the New York Yankees, Johnson was traded in 2007 to Arizona for a second stint with the Diamondbacks. The following year he recorded his 4,673rd strikeout, passing Roger Clemens for second place on the all-time strikeouts list—behind only Nolan Ryan. Johnson signed with the San Francisco Giants after the 2008 season. In 2009 he recorded the 300th victory of his career, a landmark that had been reached by only 23 other big-league pitchers. Johnson retired in 2010.

MICHAEL JORDAN

(b. 1963–)

Michael Jordan's high-leaping slam dunks inspired his nickname, "Air Jordan." He was the NBA's top scorer for a record-breaking 10 seasons. He led the Chicago Bulls to six championships in the 1990s. He was considered the most recognizable athlete in the world at the time, and his long list of product endorsements reflected his popularity.

Michael Jeffrey Jordan was born on February 17, 1963, in Brooklyn, New York. He grew up in Wilmington, North Carolina. Although he was cut from the varsity basketball team in his sophomore year of high school, he later became one of the team's star players. Jordan earned a scholarship to the University of North Carolina at Chapel Hill, where he helped lead the school's basketball team to the National Collegiate Athletic Association (NCAA) Division I championship during his freshman year. In both his sophomore and junior years, he was named the NCAA college player of the year. After his junior year he left to join the NBA (though he later returned to earn his bachelor's degree, in 1986).

Chicago Bulls star forward Michael Jordan, scoring in definitive fashion during a 1998 game against Seattle on his home court. © AP Images

Jordan was the third player chosen overall in the 1984 NBA draft, selected by the Chicago Bulls. The 6-foot, 6-inch (1.98-meter) guard quickly demonstrated the wisdom of their choice. In his first season he averaged 28.2 points per game and was named the NBA's rookie of the year. Wilt Chamberlain was the only other player to score 3,000 points in a season before Jordan did it in the 1986–87 season. Jordan won seven consecutive scoring titles from the 1986–87 season through the 1992–93 season. He led the Bulls to three consecutive NBA championships, in 1991, 1992, and 1993. He also led the U.S. basketball team to a gold medal in both the 1984 and 1992 Olympic Games.

Saying that he did not have "anything else to prove," Jordan retired from professional basketball in October 1993. In 1994 he signed on to play for a minor league baseball team, but after one season he decided to return to basketball. He rejoined the Bulls late in their 1994–95 season. After leading the team to three more back-to-back championships in 1996, 1997, and 1998, Jordan retired for the second time in January 1999.

In January 2000 Jordan bought a share of the Washington Wizards and also became the team's president of basketball operations. But he soon wanted to return to the court. He gave up his ownership and management positions with the Wizards in September 2001 in order to play on the team. In the 2002–03 season he became the first player in NBA history age 40 years or older to score more than 40 points in a game. Jordan's final retirement from basketball came in May 2003.

Jordan was named the NBA's most valuable player (MVP) in 1988, 1991, 1992, 1996, and 1998. He was also the MVP of the finals for each of his six championship seasons with the Bulls. At the time of his retirement in 2003, Jordan ranked third in career scoring, with a total of 32,292 points, behind Kareem Abdul-Jabbar and Karl Malone. Jordan's scoring average of 30.12 points per game was the highest in league history. Jordan became part owner of the NBA's Charlotte Bobcats in 2006 and took over control of the team as its majority owner in 2010. He became the first former NBA player to become a majority owner of one of the league's teams. Jordan was inducted into the Naismith Memorial Basketball Hall of Fame in September 2009.

FLORENCE GRIFFITH JOYNER

(b. 1959–d. 1998)

United States track athlete and winner of four Olympic gold medals, Florence Griffith Joyner was often called "the fastest woman alive" for setting world records in the 100- and 200-meter sprints at the 1988 Olympic Games in Seoul, South Korea. Nicknamed "FloJo," she was a trendsetter, a designer of sports clothes, a businesswoman, an actress, and the first woman chosen to head the President's Council on Physical Fitness and Sports.

Florence Delorez Griffith was born on December 21, 1959, in Los Angeles, California, the seventh of 11 children born to Robert and Florence Griffith. Florence was given the nickname "Dee Dee" to distinguish her from her mother. When she was four her mother divorced her father, and they moved from his home in the Mojave Desert to the public housing projects in the Watts section of Los Angeles. In order to stand out from her brothers and sisters Florence concentrated on running. In grade school and junior high school she competed in 50- and 70-meter dashes at events held by the Sugar Ray Robinson Youth Foundation. In her early teens she won first place two years in a row at the Jesse Owens National Youth Games. When she graduated from David Jordan High School she left a legacy of school records in the 100- and 220-yard sprints. She also began developing a personal fashion sense, sewing her own clothes and designing her own fingernail decorations and hair styles.

She enrolled in the business program at California State University (CSU) at Northridge but left after her first year and worked at a bank. Bob Kersee, her track coach from CSU, encouraged her to go back to school, and when he took a job as assistant track coach at the University of California at Los Angeles (UCLA) in 1980, she entered as a psychology major. Kersee concentrated on training her in the 200-meter sprint, and in 1982 she won the NCAA championship in that event. The following year she placed second but won the NCAA title in the 400 meters. She

57

decided to leave UCLA and focus on running with Kersee's World Class Track Club. She won a silver medal at the 1984 Los Angeles Olympics with a time of 22.04 seconds in the 200 meters. After that, she stopped competing. She spent the next two years working in Los Angeles as a customer service representative during the day and as a beautician at night.

Griffith set her sights on the 1988 Olympics with the help of Kersee, who put her on a strict regimen of diet and training, working around her job schedule. She went back into competition and won a silver medal in the 200-meter event at the World Championship in Rome, Italy. Tired of being second best, she began training even more intensely, adding weight lifting to her workouts and studying tapes of Ben Johnson's record-breaking 100-meter race. During the Olympic trials in Indiana she beat the world record in the 100-meter sprint by more than 0.25 second, the largest margin recorded until that time.

At the 1988 Seoul Summer Olympics, Griffith won the gold medal in the 100 meters with a time of 10.54 seconds, and a few days later she set another record with a gold-medal time of 21.34 seconds in the 200-meter sprint. She assisted the United States team in winning a gold medal in the 4×100-meter relay, and less than an hour later she helped the team take a silver medal in the 4×400-meter relay with the second fastest time on record: 3 minutes 15.51 seconds. The media and fans loved her for her speed and original style. She appeared on the covers of national and international magazines and on talk shows, and she received numerous offers of endorsement contracts.

In 1989 Griffith officially retired from sports competition. She married gold medalist triple-jumper Al Joyner in 1987, and in 1990 she gave birth to a daughter. Pursuing a career in entertainment, she appeared in more than 200 television shows and hosted televised track events. In 1992 she turned the Florence Griffith Joyner Youth Foundation, which she had started in 1984, into a nonprofit organization. She designed uniforms for the Indiana Pacers basketball team, sportswear for several Japanese companies, and the FloJo Olympic clothing line. Beginning in 1993 she cochaired the President's Council on Physical Fitness and Sports with Tom McMillen.

Some of the awards Griffith Joyner received were the 1988 Sullivan Trophy, the International Jesse Owens Award, the 1989 United States

U.S. track and field athlete Jackie Joyner-Kersee, clearing a hurdle during a California meet in 1993. Tony Duffy/Hulton Archive/Getty Images

Olympic Committee Award, the German Golden Camera Award, the 1989 Harvard Foundation Award, and an honorary Ph.D. from American University in Washington. She died in Mission Viejo, California, on September 21, 1998.

JACKIE JOYNER-KERSEE

(b. 1962–)

Jacqueline Joyner (named, by her grandmother, for Jacqueline Kennedy) was born on March 3, 1962, in East St. Louis, Illinois. A track-and-field livewire famous for her energy and good humor, Jackie Joyner-Kersee was widely considered the greatest woman athlete of her time.

She was the first U.S. woman to set a world record in multi-event competition and the first to break the 7,000-point barrier, with 7,148 points in the heptathlon at the 1986 Goodwill Games in Moscow. She won the Olympic gold medal in the heptathlon in 1988 and again in 1992, breaking her own record and setting a new world record with her gold-medal long jump in the 1988 Olympic Games in Seoul, South Korea. At the age of 14, Joyner won the first of four National Junior Pentathlon championships and encouraged her brother Al to begin training for the triple jump. The two later competed together for the United States.

Jackie Joyner graduated in the top 10 percent of her high school class and attended the University of California at Los Angeles on a basketball scholarship, playing as a basketball All-American and as part of the UCLA track team. It was UCLA assistant coach Bob Kersee (whom she married in 1986) who persuaded her to focus on the heptathlon in international competition. A hamstring injury troubled her in the 1983 world track and field championships in Helsinki, Finland, but she won the silver medal in the 1984 Olympic Games in Los Angeles. She received a bachelor's degree in history from UCLA in 1985.

Joyner gained her world's-best reputation in 1986 with the Goodwill Games in Moscow. In 1987 she tied the world's record in the long jump at the Pan American Games and won the heptathlon and long jump gold medals at the Rome World Championships.

Among her many honors are the Jesse Owens Award (1986 and 1987), the Sullivan Award as best amateur athlete in the United States (1986), the *Track & Field News* Athlete of the Year title (1986), the Associated Press Female Athlete of the Year (1987), *Ebony* magazine American Black Achievement award (1987), the Jim Thorpe Award (1993), and the Jackie Robinson "Robie" award (1994).

DOROTHY KAMENSHEK

(b. 1925–d. 2010)

Dorothy Kamenshek was one of the stars of women's professional baseball, who was considered a superior player at first base and at bat.

Kamenshek was born on December 21, 1925, in Cincinnati, Ohio. She showed promise as an outfielder with a local softball league by the time she was 17. A scout for the newly created All-American Girls Professional

Baseball League (AAGPBL) persuaded her to try out in Chicago. She made the league, and from 1943 to 1953 she played for the Rockford (Illinois) Peaches, starting as an outfielder but soon taking over at first base. Kamenshek's skills at first base impressed former New York Yankee Wally Pipp, as being the most accomplished he had ever seen among men or women. He once predicted that Kamenshek would be the first woman selected for the men's major leagues. In fact, a men's team from the Florida International League did attempt to recruit her in 1950, but she declined the offer, believing it was basically a publicity stunt.

During her 10-year career with the AAGPBL, she was selected for seven All-Star teams, held the league's put-out record, won the batting title two years in a row, and struck out only 81 out of 3,736 times at bat. The achievements of Kamenshek and her teammates inspired the film *A League of Their Own* (1992).

Back injuries caused Kamenshek to retire after the 1951 season. She began studying at Marquette University in Milwaukee, Wisconsin, for a physical therapy degree. In 1953 she returned to the Rockford Peaches to help boost the team's ticket sales, but she retired permanently at the end of the season. After graduating from Marquette, Kamenshek worked as a physical therapist in Michigan. She moved to California and eventually became the director of the Los Angeles Crippled Children's Services Department. She died on May 17, 2010, in Palm Desert, California.

MARIO LEMIEUX

(b. 1965–)

Mario Lemieux was born on October 5, 1965, in Montreal, Quebec, and grew up in suburban Ville Emard. His father was a construction worker. Mario and his two older brothers skated almost as soon as they could walk. After several years of playing in youth hockey leagues, Mario joined the Quebec major junior hockey league Laval Voisins in 1981. The next year he dropped out of school to concentrate on junior hockey full-time.

By June 1984 he was old enough for the NHL draft. Meanwhile, the Pittsburgh Penguins played so badly in the 1983–84 season that they got first pick in the next National Hockey League (NHL) draft. They chose Lemieux, who stood just over 6 feet, 4 inches (1.93 meters) tall and weighed more than 200 pounds (90 kilograms). Within a few years Lemieux led the Penguins to two Stanley Cup championships. He was the top NHL scorer in six different years before he retired at the age of 31.

His first year in Pittsburgh, far from home, was hard for the shy 19-year-old. He lived with a Pittsburgh family and watched television soap operas to improve his English. On the ice he was at home from the start, scoring 100 points in 73 games and earning NHL designations as Rookie of the Year and Most Valuable All-Star. He wore the number 66 in upside-down honor of the 99 worn by his hero, Wayne Gretzky.

In the 1985–86 season Lemieux scored the second highest number of points in the NHL, after Gretzky. He missed several games the next year because of a sprained knee and bronchitis. In the off-season his participation in international competition in September 1987 was a turning point for Lemieux. On Team Canada with Gretzky and other top Canadian players, he gained the confidence to become a superstar.

He scored 168 points for Pittsburgh in 1987–88, beating out Gretzky to become the league's top scorer. He was named NHL player of the year, but the Penguins still did not reach the play-offs. When Lemieux finally led his team to the play-offs in 1989, excited Pittsburgh city officials named him man of the year. He built a house to share with his Montreal girlfriend, Nathalie Asselin, whom he had met while playing for Laval.

A herniated disk, back operation, and subsequent infection kept Lemieux out of play for much of 1989–90 and 1990–91. After his return in January 1991, he led the Penguins to their first Stanley Cup championship. They won again in 1992.

Lemieux underwent an operation and radiation treatment for Hodgkin's disease, a form of cancer, in early 1993 but was playing again by March. He married Asselin that June. Recurring back pain made Lemieux miss 62 games in 1993–94, and he decided to take the next year off for his health. He played the following two seasons and then retired, saying he was tired of the clutching and grabbing that hurt the level of NHL play. He also said he had "lost a step." Other players and sports writers disagreed. Some called him the greatest hockey player ever.

GREG LEMOND

(b. 1961–)

In a physically demanding sport dominated by Europeans, cyclist Greg LeMond's back-to-back victories in cycling's most prestigious annual event, the three-week, 2,000-mile (3,200-kilometer) Tour de France, inspired many to take up the sport.

Gregory James LeMond was born on June 26, 1961, in Reno, Nevada. He began cycling competitively when he was 14 and soon became a top amateur racer. In 1978

Bicyclist Greg LeMond, smiling for the cameras during the 1992 Tour Dupont. Mike Powell/Hulton Archive/ Getty Images

he became the first American to win three medals in Olympic or world cycling competition. He turned professional in 1981 and captured the Coors Classic stage race, which went from San Francisco, Calif., to Boulder, Colo., that year.

In 1984 his third-place finish in the Tour de France was the best showing ever by a non-European. Two years later he won the event, but a near-fatal hunting accident in 1987 left him in critical condition. His career seemed to have been brought to a close, but he made an amazing recovery and came back to win the 1989 and 1990 Tour events and finished seventh in 1991. His achievements were of great interest in cycling in the United States. LeMond was honored by *Sports Illustrated* as the 1989 Sportsman of the Year.

CARL LEWIS

(b. 1961–)

Carl Lewis was born on July 1, 1961, in Birmingham, Alabama. With his victory in the long jump at the 1996 Olympics in Atlanta, Georgia, Lewis joined Al Oerter as the only other athlete to win four Olympic gold medals in the same track-and-field event. Lewis won three gold medals at the world championships in 1983 before competing in his first Olympics. At the 1984 Summer Games in Los Angeles, he equaled Jesse Owens's feat of the 1936 Olympics in Berlin by winning gold medals in the long jump, 100 meters, 200 meters, and the 4×100-meter relay.

He won gold medals in the 100 meters and long jump and silver in the 200 meters at the 1988 Summer Olympics in Seoul. At the 1992 Olympic Games in Barcelona he won a third consecutive gold in the long jump and a gold in the 4×100-meter relay. His gold medal in the long jump in 1996, at age 35, increased his Olympic career totals to nine golds and one silver. In 1997 Lewis retired from competition.

NANCY LIEBERMAN

(b. 1958–)

A pioneer in women's basketball, Nancy Lieberman recorded several unmatched accomplishments in a playing career that spanned three decades.

Nancy Lieberman was born on July 1, 1958, in Brooklyn, New York. She combined toughness and court knowledge with a natural ability to compete, in the male-dominated New York basketball scene. She entered Old Dominion University in Virginia in 1976 and led the school to consecutive Association for Intercollegiate Athletics for Women (AIAW) championships in 1978–79 and 1979–80. An intelligent and extraordinarily quick point guard, she was known for her passing and firm defense as well as her accurate shooting touch, which enabled her to average 18.1 points per game over her four-year career. She was named national player of the year twice and ended her collegiate career as Old Dominion's all-time leader in assists and steals.

At the international level, she helped lead the United States to a gold medal in the 1975 Pan American Games. She was also a member of the silver medal–winning 1976 United States Olympic team; she made the 1980 team as well, but the squad did not compete because of an American boycott of the Games.

In the early 1980s, professional basketball in the United States offered few, if any, opportunities for women. Nevertheless, after the close of her career at Old

Nancy Lieberman, posing for photos in 1990, during her pioneering career as a basketball player. Tim DeFrisco/ Hulton Archive/Getty Images

Dominion, Lieberman aspired to stay involved in the game she loved. In 1980 she was the number one draft pick of the Dallas Diamonds of the Women's Basketball League (WBL), a small women's professional league. The WBL folded in 1982, leaving its players without a professional league once again. In 1984 Lieberman was again the first draft pick of a newly created professional circuit, the Women's American Basketball Association (WABA). Because fan interest for a women's professional league still was not strong enough to generate financial success, however, the WABA was also short-lived.

Unwilling to leave the United States for Europe, where she had several offers to play professionally, Lieberman continued to look for new opportunities at home. She became the first woman to try out for a National Basketball Association (NBA) team and the first to play in a men's professional league, in 1986 with the Springfield Fame in the United States Basketball League (USBL). In 1988 Lieberman was chosen by the Washington Generals to play against the Harlem Globetrotters, making her the first woman to participate in a Harlem Globetrotters world tour. Approaching the age of 40 but still a talented player, she joined the Phoenix Mercury of the newly formed, NBA-sponsored Women's National Basketball Association (WBNA) in 1996.

Aside from her basketball career, Lieberman maintained interests in several other areas. She was a well-known public speaker on topics such as drug awareness and leadership. In addition, she established her own sports marketing company, served as tennis star Martina Navratilova's conditioning coach, and became an accomplished broadcaster. She was inducted into the Basketball Hall of Fame in 1996.

RYAN LOCHTE

(b. 1984–)

Ryan Lochte won 11 career Olympic medals, 5 of which were gold. He also set many swimming world records. He attended the University of Florida, where he won seven National Collegiate Athletic Association swimming titles, including three individual titles in 2006.

Ryan Lochte was born on August 3, 1984, in Rochester, New York. He first attracted international attention at the 2004 Olympic Games in Athens, Greece, where he earned a gold medal as a member of the victorious American 4 × 200-meter freestyle relay team and claimed silver in the 200-meter individual medley (IM), behind fellow American Michael Phelps.

At the 2006 Fédération Internationale de Natation (FINA) short-course (25-meter) world championships, Lochte set world records in the 100-meter backstroke, 200-meter backstroke, and 200-meter IM. He then set a long-course (50-meter) world record in the 200-meter backstroke at the FINA world championships in 2007.

At the 2008 Olympic Games in Beijing, China, Lochte won a gold medal in the 200-meter backstroke, setting a new global standard of 1 minute 53.94 seconds. He earned yet another gold and world record in the 4 × 200-meter freestyle relay, and he finished with bronzes in both the 200-meter and 400-meter IM.

In 2009 and 2010 Lochte continued his string of impressive performances. At the 2009 FINA world championships, he broke Phelps's world record in the 200-meter IM and also won the 400-meter IM. He won six gold medals to Phelps's five at the 2010 Pan Pacific championships. Later that year Lochte collected an unmatched seven medals at the FINA short-course worlds. He won all five of his individual races and two, the 200-meter and 400-meter IM, in world-record time. He also sparked the Americans to a come-from-behind victory in the 4 × 100-meter medley relay. He also won silver as part of the American 4 × 200-meter freestyle relay team.

At the 2011 FINA world championships, Lochte won five gold medals. He twice bested Phelps in head-to-head competition at the 200-meter freestyle event and the 200-meter IM. In the latter race, Lochte set the first world record since FINA banned high-performance non-textile swimsuits in January 2010, breaking his own world record (set in a high-tech suit) with a new global standard of 1 minute 54 seconds. Showcasing his amazing ability to adapt, he also collected wins in the 200-meter backstroke and the 400-meter IM and helped power the American team to gold in the 4 × 200-meter freestyle relay.

Lochte and Phelps again engaged in high-profile showdowns at the 2012 Olympic Games in London, England. Lochte swam to victory in the 400-meter IM at the outset of the swimming competition, while Phelps finished the race in fourth place. In the 200-meter IM, however, Lochte finished a close second to Phelps. The two competitors joined forces in two relay events, winning gold in the 4 × 200-meter freestyle relay and silver in the 4 × 100-meter freestyle relay. Lochte also won a bronze medal in the 200-meter backstroke.

GREG LOUGANIS

(b. 1960–)

Greg Louganis won gold medals in the springboard and platform events at the 1984 and 1988 Olympics, the first man to do so in consecutive games in more than 50 years. As a member of the United States

Diver Greg Louganis, proudly displaying one of two gold medals he won during the 1988 Olympics in Seoul, South Korea.
AFP/Getty Images

national diving team from 1976 to 1988, he won first-place titles in 47 United States indoor and outdoor competitions, 18 Olympic trials, and 41 international competitions in the 12-year span of his career.

Greg Louganis was born on Jan. 29, 1960, in San Diego, California, to young parents who gave him up for adoption. When he was less than a year old he was adopted by Peter and Frances Louganis of El Cajon, California. They gave him the name Gregory Efthimios Louganis. His early life was difficult. He was shy, had a stutter, had difficulty keeping up in school because of dyslexia, and was afraid of heights. In addition, he and his adopted sister Despina took dancing and gymnastic lessons, which were far from what were considered "real" sports at the time.

When Louganis started using his athletic skills in the family pool, however, he found his calling. By the time he was 11 he was an Amateur Athletic Union (AAU) Junior Olympic diving champion. Four years later Sammy Lee, a gold-medal diver in the 1948 and 1952 Olympics, began coaching Louganis for the 1976 games in Montreal, Que. There, Louganis took sixth place in the 3-meter springboard event and won a silver medal in 10-meter platform diving at the age of 16. In 1978 he began attending the University of Miami in Florida and started his streak of 1-meter and 3-meter National Collegiate Athletic Association (NCAA) titles, which he won every year that he competed. He was winning titles in national and world competitions. Louganis was heavily favored for the upcoming 1980 Olympics in Moscow, U.S.S.R. However, the United States government's decision to boycott the Summer Games to protest the recent Soviet invasion of Afghanistan prevented Louganis and his fellow American athletes from competing.

In 1981 he transferred to the University of California at Irvine and started training with Ron O'Brien, the coach of a champion-producing swim club. Three years later Louganis graduated with a bachelor's degree in drama and was ready for the next Olympics. At the 1984 Los Angeles, Calif., Summer Games he won gold medals in the 3-meter springboard and 10-meter platform events. In the platform event, he received perfect scores of 10 from seven judges, and with his 710.91 score he became the first diver to score more than 700 points in competition.

In recognition of his achievements Louganis received the Sullivan Award for amateur athletes. He was entered in the Olympic Hall of Fame in 1985, and a year later he was awarded the Jesse Owens International Trophy. Louganis wrote a book about his life, *A Single Obsession*, with author James Babbit in 1986.

There were new chapters to write when Louganis became the first athlete to repeat gold medal performances in both diving events at the 1988 Olympic Games in Seoul, South Korea. Louganis triumphed over younger contestants by performing more difficult dives and achieving perfect execution, even after hitting the back of his head on the diving board.

After the Olympics Louganis pursued a career in theater, acting in off-Broadway productions. He also promoted Speedo products. In 1995 he published another autobiography, *Breaking the Surface*, with Eric Mareus. In the book he frankly discussed his life as a gay, HIV-positive athlete, including the dispute over his knowledge that he had tested positive for the AIDS virus before the 1988 Olympics. The Olympic committee though, did not require testing for HIV and there had been no known cases of infection transmitted in the course of sports activity.

PEYTON MANNING

(b. 1976–)

Peyton Manning was named most valuable player (MVP) of the National Football League (NFL) four times in his first 12 seasons. He led the Indianapolis Colts to a Super Bowl victory in 2007.

Peyton Williams Manning was born on March 24, 1976, in New Orleans, Louisiana. He was introduced to football from a very young age. His father, Archie Manning, was a star quarterback with the New Orleans Saints. (Younger brother Eli also became an NFL quarterback.) Manning attended the University of Tennessee, where he was the starting quarterback for four years. He earned the Sullivan Award as the country's top amateur athlete in 1996, was selected a first-team All-American in 1997, and finished his collegiate career in 1998 as Tennessee's career passing leader.

Manning was drafted first overall by the Indianapolis Colts in 1998. After struggling somewhat in his rookie season, he helped the Colts in 1999 to win the franchise's first division title since 1987. In 2000 Manning threw for 4,413 yards and 33 touchdowns to finish among the NFL's leading passers. Three years later he shared the league's MVP award with Steve McNair of the Tennessee Titans. Manning won the MVP honor outright in 2004 with a sensational performance that included 49 touchdown passes, an NFL record for a single season (his touchdown record was broken by Tom Brady in 2007).

During the 2005 season, Manning led the Colts to victories in their first 13 games. Although considered one of the favorites to win the Super Bowl, the team lost in the divisional play-offs. Some questioned Manning's ability to win a championship, but in the 2006 season he silenced his critics. He threw for 4,397 yards—the seventh time in his career he had passed for more than 4,000 yards, breaking Dan Marino's record—and helped the Colts defeat the Chicago Bears in Super Bowl XLI. For his performance, which included 25 completed passes for 247 yards, Manning was named the game's

MVP. In 2008 and 2009 he won his third and fourth league MVP awards. After the 2009 season Manning led the Colts to the Super Bowl once again, but his team lost to the New Orleans Saints.

Manning once again earned Pro Bowl accolades after leading the Colts to a 10th consecutive play-off berth in 2010. He had neck surgery the following off-season (the third procedure on his neck in a 19-month span), and a difficult recovery forced him to miss the entire 2011 season, which brought his streak of consecutive regular-season starts to an end at 208 games (the second highest total for a quarterback in NFL history). Without Manning, the Colts struggled to a 2–14 record. The team released Manning in March 2012 to avoid paying the injured quarterback a $28 million bonus and to begin rebuilding around a nucleus of younger players. Manning then signed a five-year contract with the Denver Broncos.

DIEGO MARADONA

(b. 1960–)

O ne of the most famous soccer (association football) players of the 1980s, and possibly the entire profession, Diego Maradona became a hero to the poor in his native Argentina. He led teams from Argentina, Spain, and Italy to championship wins, including Argentina's 1986 World Cup success. He played 490 official club games during his 21-year professional career, scoring 259 goals.

Diego Armando Maradona was born on Oct. 30, 1960, in Lanus, Buenos Aires, Argentina. Maradona was interested in soccer from a young age and played for a boys' team when he was only eight years old. The team won 136 games in a row and the national championship. He competed with the Argentinos Juniors at age 14 and made his division debut in 1976. Four months later, at the age of 16, Maradona joined the national team. He was the youngest Argentine to ever play on a national team. In 1979 he led his team to a Junior World Cup victory.

Maradona moved to the Boca Juniors in 1981 and helped them win the championship. He then went to Europe, where he would play for the next 10 seasons. He spent his first two years in Barcelona, winning the Spanish Cup in 1983, and then moved to Napoli. Maradona greatly improved the quality of the Napoli team, which made him a hero to the poor in southern Italy. Napoli won the league and cup titles in 1987 and the league title again in 1990.

A loyal Argentine, Maradona played on his homeland's World Cup teams in 1982, 1986, 1990, and 1994. In the quarterfinal of the 1986 World Cup, he scored the famous "Hand of God" goal. Maradona had illegally hit the ball with his hand, but the referee mistakenly thought he had used his head (which is allowed). He also played on the winning teams in the South American cup in 1987 and 1989.

Maradona's career began to decline when he was banned from playing soccer for 15 months for using drugs in 1991. He was sent home from the 1994 World Cup after drug tests showed he was using a drug called ephedrine, which illegally improves performance. Maradona continued to play soccer in Spain and Argentina before retiring in 1997. He served as head coach of the Argentine national team from 2008 to 2010.

MARTA

(b. 1986–)

Marta is a Brazilian athlete who is widely considered the greatest female football (soccer) player of all time. Marta was a five-time winner of the Fédération Internationale de Football Association (FIFA) World Player of the Year award (2006–10).

Marta, christened Marta Vieira da Silva, was born on February 19, 1986, in Dois Riachos, Brazil. Prevented from playing football with her male peers because of her gender, Marta began honing her skills as a young girl by kicking abandoned deflated footballs and improvised balls made up of wadded grocery bags through the streets of her small town. She eventually joined a local boys' junior team, when she was discovered at age 14 by a scout from Vasco da Gama, a renowned men's football club in Rio de Janeiro that was looking to begin a women's team. Thereafter she played on women's teams, beginning

Brazilian soccer player Marta (far right) *celebrates making a goal against the United States in the quarterfinals of the FIFA Women's World Cup in 2011.* Martin Rose/Getty Images

with Vasco, until it folded a few years later, and then with Santa Cruz in Brazil before joining Sweden's Umeå IK in 2004.

Marta first gained widespread notice during her time with Umeå, which she led to the 2004 Union of European Football Associations (UEFA) Women's Cup (now known as the Women's Champions League) title and helped to reach the finals in that competition in 2007 and 2008. Marta also helped Umeå capture four consecutive Damallsvenskan (Sweden's highest level of women's domestic football) championships between 2005 and 2008, as well as a Swedish Cup title in 2007. Marta scored a remarkable 111 goals in 103 league games during her five seasons with Umeå as she led the league in goals over three seasons (2004, 2005, and 2008).

She left Europe in 2009 to sign with the Los Angeles Sol of Women's Professional Soccer (WPS). Marta was named WPS Most Valuable Player (MVP) in 2009, but the struggling Los Angeles franchise folded, and she moved within the WPS to join the FC Gold Pride of Santa Clara, California. She led the Gold Pride to a WPS title (taking home a second league MVP award) in 2010, and she won a second WPS championship in 2011 as a member of the Western New York Flash. During the WPS off-seasons in 2009 and 2010, Marta played with Santos FC in her home country. When the WPS suspended operations in 2012, Marta returned to Sweden as a member of Tyresö FF.

Marta established herself as the greatest female footballer of her generation primarily through her feats as a member of the Brazilian women's national team. She made her international football debut in 2002 as a member of Brazil's under-20 Women's World Cup team. The following year she joined the senior national squad and scored three goals at the 2003 FIFA Women's World Cup, where Brazil was eliminated in the quarterfinals. At the 2007 Women's World Cup, she won the Golden Boot by scoring seven goals during the tournament and led Brazil to a second-place finish. In 2011 Marta increased her career Cup goal tally to 14, which tied Germany's Birgit Prinz for most Women's World Cup goals of all time, but the Brazilian national team was again eliminated in the Cup quarterfinals. Marta also helped Brazil capture silver medals at the 2004 Athens and 2008 Beijing Olympic Games.

BOB MATHIAS

(b. 1930–d. 2006)

In 1948, at the age of 17, Bob Mathias became the youngest person to win a gold medal in the Olympic decathlon. Four years later he became the first person to win the decathlon at two different Olympics.

Robert Bruce Mathias was born in the farming town of Tulare, California, on November 17, 1930. He suffered from anemia as a child and turned to sports to gain strength. As a high school athlete, he excelled in football and basketball as well as track and field. After winning the high and low hurdles at the California state high school track meet in 1948, he began training for the decathlon, a tough series of 10 different sporting events spread over two days. Mathias won the decathlon event at the Pacific Coast games in Pasadena, California, then went on to triumph at the 1948 U.S. national championships, which qualified him for the Olympic Games that year in London.

At the end of the first day of decathlon competition in London, Mathias was in third place, but a strong discus throw of 44 meters (144 feet) on the second day helped put him into the lead, and he held on to win the gold. Mathias received the 1948 James E. Sullivan Award for outstanding amateur athletic achievement. At the 1952 Olympics in Helsinki, Finland, he again won the decathlon, setting a new record for the event with 7,887 points. Altogether, Mathias entered and won 11 decathlon competitions in his career.

Mathias graduated from Stanford University (B.A., 1953), where he played fullback on the football team. After his Olympic victories, he acted in several films, including *The Bob Mathias Story* (1954). He later went into politics, serving four terms in the U.S. House of Representatives (1967–75) as a Republican from the 18th District of California. In 1974 Mathias was among the first group of athletes named to the National Track and Field Hall of Fame. He served as director of the U.S. Olympic Training Center from 1977 to 1983, the year he was inducted into the U.S. Olympic Hall of Fame. Mathias died on September 2, 2006, in Fresno, California.

WILLIE MAYS

(b. 1931–)

Willie Howard Mays was born on May 6, 1931, in Westfield, Alabama. Mays was an outstanding baseball player known for both his batting and his fielding. He ranks among the all-time leaders in home runs, hits, runs scored, and runs batted in (RBI). He was also known for his spectacular leaping and diving catches. Many consider him to have been the best all-around player in the history of the game.

In 1948, while he was still in high school, he joined the Birmingham Black Barons of the Negro National League. The New York Giants of the National League (NL) bought his contract when he graduated from high school in 1950. After two seasons in the minor leagues, Mays went to the Giants in 1951 and was named Rookie of the Year at the end of that season.

After serving in the U.S. Army for two years, Mays returned to baseball for the 1954 season. He led the league in hitting (.345) and had 41 home runs, helping the Giants win the NL pennant and the World Series. In 1966 his two-year contract with the Giants (who had moved to San Francisco in 1958) gave him the highest salary of any baseball player of that time. He was traded to the New York Mets midseason in 1972 and retired after the 1973 season. Late in his career he played in the infield, mainly at first base. Mays retired with 660 home runs, 3,283 hits, 2,062 runs scored, and 1,903 RBI. He led the league in home runs in 1955, 1962, and 1964–65, won 12 consecutive Gold Gloves (1957–68), and appeared in 24 All-Star Games. He was elected to the Baseball Hall of Fame in 1979.

Willie Mays, nicknamed the "Say Hey Kid," posing for a portrait while with the San Francisco Giants in 1962. Louis Requena/ Major League Baseball/Getty Images

LIONEL MESSI

(b. 1987–)

Lionel Messi was named Fédération Internationale de Football Association (FIFA) world player of the year in 2009, 2010, 2011, and 2012.

Lionel Andrés Messi, also called Leo Messi, was on born June 24, 1987, in Rosario, Argentina. Messi started playing football as a boy and in 1995 joined the youth team of Newell's Old Boys (a Rosario-based top-division football club). Messi's remarkable skills gained the attention of major clubs on both sides of the Atlantic. At age 13 Messi and his family moved to Barcelona, and he began playing for FC Barcelona's under-14 team. He scored 21 goals in 14 games for the junior team, and he quickly graduated through the higher-level teams until at age 16 he was given his informal debut with FC Barcelona in a friendly match.

In the 2004–05 season Messi, then 17, became the youngest official player and goal scorer in the Spanish La Liga (the country's highest division of football). Messi stood only 5 feet, 7 inches (1.7 meters) tall and weighed 148 pounds (67 kg), but he was strong, well-balanced, and

FC Barcelona star Lionel Messi (front) *shoots on goal during a 2012 La Liga match in Barcelona.* Jasper Juinen/Getty Images

flexible on the field. Naturally left-footed, quick, and precise in control of the ball, Messi was a keen pass distributor and could readily make his way through packed defenses. In 2005 he was granted Spanish citizenship, an honor greeted with mixed feelings by the fiercely Catalan supporters of Barcelona. The next year Messi and Barcelona won the Champions League (the European club championship) title.

Messi's play continued to rapidly improve over the years, and by 2008 he was one of the most dominant players in the world, finishing second to Manchester United's Cristiano Ronaldo in the voting for the 2008 FIFA World Player of the Year. In early 2009 Messi capped off a spectacular 2008–09 season by helping FC Barcelona capture the club's first "treble" (winning three major European club titles in one season): the team won the La Liga championship, the Copa del Rey (Spain's major domestic cup), and the Champions League title. He scored 38 goals in 51 matches during that season, and he bested Ronaldo in the balloting for FIFA World Player of the Year honors by a record margin. During the 2009–10 season Messi scored 34 goals in domestic games as Barcelona repeated as La Liga champions. He earned the Golden Shoe award as Europe's leading scorer, and he was named the 2010 world player of the year (the award was renamed the FIFA Ballon d'Or that year).

Messi led Barcelona to La Liga and Champions League titles the following season, which helped him capture an unprecedented third consecutive world player of the year award. In March 2012 he netted his 233rd goal for Barcelona, becoming the club's all-time leading scorer when only 24 years old. He finished Barcelona's 2011–12 season (which included another Copa del Rey win) with 73 goals in all competitions, breaking Gerd Müller's 39-year-old record for single-season goals in a major European football league.

His landmark season led to his being named the 2012 world player of the year, which made Messi the first player to win the honor four times. His 46 La Liga goals in 2012–13 led the league, and Barcelona captured another domestic top-division championship that season.

Despite his dual citizenship and professional success in Spain, Messi's ties with his homeland remained strong, and he was a key member of various Argentine national teams from 2005. He played on Argentina's victorious 2005 FIFA World Youth Championship squad, represented the country in the 2006 World Cup finals, and scored two goals in five matches as Argentina won the gold medal at the Beijing 2008 Olympic Games. Messi helped Argentina reach the 2010 World Cup quarterfinals, where the team was eliminated by Germany for the second consecutive time in World Cup play.

In 2011, Messi won the FIFA Ballon d'Or yet again, and also surpassed Gerd Müller's record of most goals scored by an individual in a single European season.

CHERYL MILLER

(b. 1964–)

One of the greatest players in the history of women's basketball, Cheryl Miller was credited with both popularizing the game as well as taking it to a higher level of play.

Cheryl Miller was born on Jan. 3, 1964, in Riverside, California. While growing up in Southern California, she displayed extraordinary talent on the basketball court. She stayed close to her family by choosing to attend college at the University of Southern California (USC), where she quickly became a star. In 1983, her first season at USC, Miller burst onto the national scene by leading the Trojans to the National Collegiate Athletic Association (NCAA) women's basketball championship. Although just a freshman, she was selected as the Most Valuable Player (MVP) of the NCAA tournament because of her ability to dominate games with her all-around athleticism. In addition to having a shooting touch that made her dangerous from anywhere on the court, Miller was a feared defender and a leading rebounder. In 1984 she led USC back to the championship tournament and to another national title. She was named MVP of the NCAA tournament for the second consecutive year.

Miller followed up her two NCAA championship seasons by leading the United States women's team to its first Olympic gold medal in the 1984 Summer Games in Los Angeles. After completing her career at USC, Miller returned to the international arena. In 1986 she led American teams to titles at the women's World Basketball Championship in Moscow and at the Goodwill Games, in which the United States defeated the Soviet Union to secure the gold medal.

When she left USC, Miller was widely considered the best women's basketball player in the school's history. She earned All-America honors in each of her four seasons and was a three-time NCAA player of the year selection (1984–86). In her 128-game career, Miller established herself among the all-time NCAA leaders with 3,018 points (23.6 per game) and 1,534 rebounds (12.0 per game). At the close of her collegiate career, she was second in NCAA tournament career scoring with 333 points (20.8 per game) and first in career rebounding with 170 (10.6 per game). Miller was named woman athlete of the year by the ESPN sports network in 1985, she won the 1986 YWCA Silver Achievement Award, and became the first woman ever to be nominated for the prestigious Sullivan Award in 1986. She was the first USC basketball player—male or female—to have her jersey number retired by the university.

Miller returned to her alma mater in 1993 as head coach of USC's women's basketball team. During her two years at the helm, the Trojans compiled a 44–14 record and won the 1994 Pacific-10 conference title. In 1995 she left coaching to become a commentator for the American Broadcasting Company (ABC) before joining Turner Sports as an analyst and reporter for NBA coverage on the TNT and TBS networks. In 1996 Miller became the first female analyst to broadcast a nationally televised men's professional basketball game.

In 1997, upon the establishment of a new women's professional basketball league, the Women's National Basketball Association, Miller returned to the court as head coach and general manager of the Phoenix Mercury. She also was known for representing many charitable organizations during her career, including the Los Angeles Literacy Campaign; the American Lung, Diabetes, and Cancer Associations; and the Muscular Dystrophy Association. She was inducted into the Basketball Hall of Fame in 1995.

JOE MONTANA

(b. 1956–)

As one of the greatest U.S. professional football quarterbacks of all time, Joe Montana led the San Francisco 49ers to four Super Bowl victories and was named the Super Bowl's Most Valuable Player three times. He also ranks among the all-time leaders in passing yards and touchdown passes. His remarkable ability to bring his team to victory from the brink of defeat during the final moments of the game became known as the Montana Magic.

Joseph Clifford Montana was born on June 11, 1956, in New Eagle, Pennsylvania. An only child, Joe was raised in nearby Monongahela,

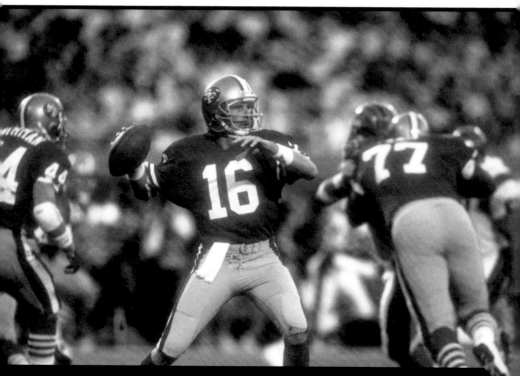

Joe Montana (No. 16) prepares to pass during the San Francisco 49s' 1989 Super Bowl win over the Cincinnati Bengals, in Miami, Florida. Mike Powell/ Hulton Archive/Getty Images

Pennsylvania, a middle-class neighborhood located near Pittsburgh, and his father encouraged him to get involved in sports. Montana demonstrated his athletic abilities at an early age, pitching three perfect games and batting .500 in Little League baseball, and high jumping 6 feet 9 inches (2.06 meters) at age 15. In high school, Montana continued to excel in sports and was a member of the football team, as well as the basketball team—for which he played every position. He was offered a basketball scholarship, but he turned down the scholarship in favor of the opportunity to play football for the Fighting Irish at the University of Notre Dame.

Montana began his college football career in 1974 as the seventh-string quarterback and moved up to third-string in 1977. After leading his team to three fourth-quarter comeback victories, he was made the starting quarterback and led the Irish to a national championship that year and Cotton Bowl victories in 1978 and 1979. He graduated from Notre Dame with a bachelor of business administration degree in marketing.

Montana's professional football career began when he was selected by the San Francisco 49ers in the third round of the 1979 National Football League (NFL) draft. Because of his modest build and the questionable strength of his throwing arm, Montana, at 6 feet, 2 inches (1.87 meters), and 195 pounds (88.45 kilograms), was often mistaken for a punter. In 1982 Montana led the 49ers to their first world championship with a victory in Super Bowl XVI. He and the 49ers returned to the Super Bowl again to become four-time champions with victories in Super Bowls XIX (1985), XXIII (1989), and XXIV (1990). Because of his outstanding performance, he was named the most valuable player of Super Bowls XVI, XIX, and XXIV. Montana was known for his calm, controlled leadership on the field when under intense pressure.

Due to his injured throwing arm, Montana missed the entire 1991 season but returned to play at the end of 1992. In 1993 he was traded to the Kansas City Chiefs, for whom he quarterbacked through the 1994 season—leading them to the play-offs both seasons. In 1994 Montana achieved more than 40,000 career passing yards, becoming only the fifth quarterback to do so. Following his second season with Kansas City, Montana retired from professional football at the age of 38.

Montana's outstanding career includes 31 fourth-quarter comeback victories, 11 play-off games, and 9 divisional championships. He was voted to the Pro Bowl eight times and was named All-NFL and All-NFC three and five times, respectively. Upon his retirement, Montana ranked fourth among all-time leading passers with 40,551 passing yards, 5,391 attempts, and 273 touchdown passes. He ranked third all-time with 3,409 completions, and his career passer rating of 92.3 ranked second all-time. On December 15, 1997, the San Francisco 49ers retired Montana's uniform jersey number 16. Montana was enshrined in the Pro Football Hall of Fame in Canton, Ohio, on July 29, 2000.

STAN MUSIAL

(b. 1920–d. 2013)

Stanley Frank Musial was born in Donora, Pennsylvania, on November 21, 1920. U.S. Musial, known as Stan the Man, won seven National League (NL) batting championships and three Most Valuable Player (MVP) awards during a 22-year playing career with the St. Louis Cardinals. By the end of his career, he had established himself as one of baseball's greatest hitters.

As a youth he was successful in both baseball and basketball, and he signed his first professional baseball contract while in high school. A left-handed batter and thrower, Musial began his career as a pitcher but developed a sore arm and switched to the outfield while still in the minor leagues. He quickly worked his way up through the Cardinals' minor league system and made his major league debut in 1941. The following year he became a full-time player for St. Louis, where he teamed with Terry Moore and Enos Slaughter to form what would become one of the finest offensive and defensive outfield combinations in baseball history and played a significant role in the team's 1942 World Series victory.

In 1943, at the age of 22, Musial led the NL in hits (220) and batting average (.357) and won the league's MVP award. After helping the Cardinals win another World Series title in 1944, he enlisted in the U.S. Navy during World War II. Returning to baseball in 1946, he won a second MVP award after batting .365 as the Cardinals captured their third World Series championship in five years. Musial had his greatest season statistically in 1948 as he posted career-high (and league-leading) totals in batting average (.376), hits (230), runs (135), and runs batted in (131), which resulted in a third NL MVP award.

In the 1950s the Cardinals had little success as a team, but Musial thrived as an individual, leading the league in batting average four times (1950–52, 1957), in runs three times (1951–52, 1954), and in hits once (1952).

Musial retired in 1963. In 10,972 at bats over the course of 3,026 games, he recorded 3,630 hits for a career batting average of .331. His total runs batted in were 1,951. In addition to his batting prowess, he led the league's outfielders in fielding in 1949, 1954, and 1961. Following his playing days, he stayed with the Cardinals organization as a member of the front office, serving as general manager in 1967, when he oversaw a World Series championship. He also directed the president's physical fitness program from 1964 through 1967. He was elected to the Baseball Hall of Fame in 1969. In 2011 Musial was awarded the Presidential Medal of Freedom. He died on January 19, 2013, in Ladue, Missouri.

RAFAEL NADAL

(b. 1986–)

Best known for his skill on a clay court, Spanish tennis player Rafael Nadal ranked among the game's top competitors in the early 21st century. He won a record eight career French Open championships.

Rafael Nadal was born on June 3, 1986, in Manacor, a town on the Spanish island of Majorca. He began playing tennis at the age of four, guided by an uncle, Toni Nadal, who remained his coach after he turned professional in 2001. As a pro player, Nadal progressed quickly, breaking into the top 50 in the world by 2003. In 2004 he played an important role in Spain's victory over the United States in the Davis Cup final. Toppling Andy Roddick, who was then number two in the world in a four-set opening-day singles clash, Nadal became the youngest player (at 18 years 6 months) in the history of the international team competition to win a singles match for a victorious country.

Over the next several years Nadal developed a notable rivalry with world number one Roger Federer of Switzerland. In 2005 Nadal triumphed at his French Open debut (at Roland Garros), when he upset Federer in the semifinals. The following year he secured his second straight French Open championship, this time besting Federer in the final. In 2007 Nadal extended his victories on clay surfaces to a record 81 consecutive matches before losing to Federer in May. He won the French Open again in 2007 and 2008, and, with his victory over Federer in the 2008 Wimbledon final, he became the first man since Bjorn Borg (1980) to capture the French Open and Wimbledon titles in the same year. In August 2008 Nadal won the men's singles gold medal at the Olympic Games in Beijing, China, and he took over the number one world ranking from Federer in the same month.

Nadal won the Australian Open championship in 2009 and at the end of that season helped Spain sweep the Czech Republic in the Davis Cup final. In 2010 he again won both the French Open and Wimbledon championships and also claimed the U.S. Open title, thus completing a career Grand Slam by having won each of the four major tennis tournaments.

Nadal won yet another showdown with Federer when they met in the 2011 French Open final. He then proceeded to lose three consecutive Grand Slam finals to Serbian tennis player Novak Djokovic before prevailing over Djokovic in the final of the 2012 French Open to secure his seventh title at Roland Garros. By this, Nadal broke the record of six French Open titles that he had shared with Borg. Nadal added another French Open title in 2013, becoming the first man to win the same Grand Slam singles event eight times.

STEVE NASH

(b. 1974–)

S teve Nash is a South African-born Canadian basketball player who is considered to be one of the greatest point guards in National Basketball Association (NBA) history. For three seasons (2004–05 to 2006–07), Steve Nash was the most important, if not best, player in the NBA.

Stephen John Nash was born on February 7, 1974 in Johannesburg, South Africa. In 2004 he joined the Phoenix Suns as a free agent, brought in to lead the run-and-gun offense of head coach Mike D'Antoni. The partnership was inspired and Nash captured the NBA Most Valuable Player (MVP) award in 2005 and 2006. He might have done so in 2007 too, if not for fears that he was getting too decorated.

Nash was raised in Victoria, British Columbia—not exactly a basketball hotbed—and was recruited by a single American college, Santa Clara University. Santa Clara was not known for its basketball prowess, but it did not take long for Nash to arrive on the national scene. In 1992–93, Nash's first year with the program, Santa Clara upset the Powerhouse University of Arizona in the National Collegiate Athletic Association championship tournament. By the time he graduated in 1996, he was regarded highly enough to be picked 15th overall in the NBA draft by the Suns.

Nash did not really get a chance to show his best play in Phoenix. The point guard position was taken by, in succession, Sam Cassell, Kevin Johnson, and Jason Kidd, all bigger names and more established players. When Nash was traded to the Dallas Mavericks in 1998, he began to develop upon his promise. In 2000–01 Nash exploded with star numbers (15.6 points and 7.3 assists per game), and at the same time, teammate Dirk Nowitzki emerged as one of the league's great scorers. They led the Mavericks to the play-offs that season and would do so again every subsequent year that Nash was in Dallas. The Mavericks, coached by the eccentric Don Nelson, were a high-scoring, versatile squad. While Nowitzki was the team's go-to scorer, Nash was the engine that made it all go.

Nevertheless, owner Mark Cuban decided that Nash was over-the-hill at age 30 and refused to match a free-agent offer from Phoenix following the 2003–04 season. As it turned out, Cuban could not have been more wrong and Nash could not have taken over as Phoenix's star at a better time. Recent rule changes had greatly reduced the amount of contact a defender was allowed to make around the perimeter. Nash had a strange gift for driving into the key and discovering new, seemingly impossible, passing lanes, and the new rules made Nash's approach more effective than ever before as he led the league in assists per game five times (including his career-high 11.6 assists per game in 2006–07) during the eight years of his second stint with the Suns.

The Suns advanced to the Western Conference finals in 2004–05. The team lost aggressive forward Amar'e Stoudemire to injury in the next preseason and yet, despite the absence of one of the league's best young players, once again appeared in the conference finals in 2005–06. Nash himself was even better, averaging a personal-best 18.8 points per game. In 2006–07, with Stoudemire back, the Suns dominated the NBA for much of the season, finishing with the second best record in the league (61–21). However, giving Nash a third consecutive MVP would have put him in the same class as all-time greats Bill Russell, Wilt Chamberlain, and Larry Bird. The voters balked. He finished second in the MVP voting to Nowitzki. The Suns then had a disappointing postseason, losing in the conference semifinals.

The Suns acquired an aging and relatively immobile Shaquille O'Neal during the following season, a move that cramped Nash's free-flowing style. Nevertheless, he was selected to his sixth All-Star Game and continued to excel individually even as the Suns went into decline. In 2012 he was traded to the Los Angeles Lakers, where he joined with fellow superstars Kobe Bryant and Dwight Howard in search of his elusive championship ring.

MARTINA NAVRATILOVA

(b. 1956–)

Czech-born U.S. citizen Martina Navratilova was a leading competitor in the open era of tennis. She won a million-dollar Grand Slam bonus in 1984. Under a temporary rule change, players became eligible for the bonus by winning the four Grand Slam victories in succession, rather than in a season. After winning the United States and Australian opens in 1983, Navratilova qualified for the special prize by taking Wimbledon and the French Open the next year.

Navratilova was born in Prague on October 18, 1956. Ranked number one in Czechoslovakia from 1972 to 1975, she achieved international prominence as the leader of the Czech team that won the 1975 Federation Cup. Afterward she defected to the United States and became a citizen in 1981.

An bird's eye view of Martina Navratilova, serving during a 1991 U.S. Open match. Dan Smith/Hulton Archive/Getty Images

In 1979 Navratilova was ranked top woman tennis player in the world, a ranking she achieved again in 1982 and maintained through 1986. A left-handed player, she amassed a remarkable record of wins in both singles and doubles. In 1983 her ratio of wins to losses (86 to 1) set a new record for percentage of wins. In 1987 Navratilova won her fourth United States Open singles and her ninth Wimbledon crown.

One of Navratilova's frequent opponents on the court was Chris Evert. Until Evert's retirement in 1990, their contrasting styles of play made them great crowd pleasers. In late 1991 Navratilova broke her longtime rival's career record of 1,309 match victories and 157 tournament titles. On winning her 158th title in 1992 in Chicago, Navratilova had won more championships than any other player, male or female, in the history of tennis. She retired from singles play after the 1994 season, having won 167 titles in all.

Over the next two years Navratilova competed in only a handful of doubles events, and from 1997 to 1999 she did not play on tour. In 2000, however, she returned to professional play, competing in the doubles event at several tournaments, including Wimbledon. That same year she was inducted into the Tennis Hall of Fame. In 2003 she won the mixed doubles (with Leander Paes) at Wimbledon to tie Billie Jean King for most Wimbledon titles overall (20). With the victory, Navratilova, age 46, also became the oldest player to win at Wimbledon. After winning the mixed doubles at the U.S. Open in 2006, she retired from competitive play. Her career totals include 59 Grand Slam titles: 18 singles, 31 doubles, and 10 mixed doubles.

Navratilova's autobiography, *Martina* (written with George Vecsey), was published in 1985. She also wrote, with Liz Nickles, a series of mysteries centered on the character Jordan Myles, a former tennis champion turned sleuth. *The Total Zone* (1994) was followed by *Breaking Point* (1996) and *Killer Instinct* (1997).

JACK NICKLAUS

(b. 1940–)

Golfer Jack Nicklaus, nicknamed "the Golden Bear," following the trajectory of a shot during a 1986 tournament in Surrey, England. Simon Bruty/Hulton Archive/Getty Images

Jack Nicklaus was the only golfer to win three career Grand Slams (winning all four of the top professional tournaments at least three times each). At 21 he was the youngest player since Bobby Jones to win the United States Open, and at 46 he was the oldest to win the Masters. When he became golf's first 5-million-dollar man in 1988, no other player had won as many major titles. Many hailed him as the greatest golfer of the 20th century.

Jack William Nicklaus was born in Columbus, Ohio, on January 21, 1940. Nicklaus's father, a pharmacist, took up golf as therapy for an ankle injury, and Jack tagged along. He played his first round when he was 10. In 1959, while a student at Ohio State University, he became the youngest golfer in 50 years to win the United States Amateur. During that year he was defeated only once in 30 matches. He won the Amateur again in 1961 before he turned professional at an exhibition on Dec. 30, 1961. Nicklaus won no tournaments during his first five months as a pro, but his legendary career took off in June 1962 when he defeated Arnold Palmer at the United States Open. He won that title again in 1967, 1972, and 1980.

There were six lean years without a major victory and two years with no victory at all before Nicklaus won his sixth Masters in 1986 by shooting a final-round 65; the other five were in 1963, 1965, 1966, 1972, and 1975. He won the Professional Golfers' Association (PGA) championship five times (1963, 1971, 1973, 1975, and 1980), and the British Open three times (1966, 1970, and 1978). Nicklaus joined the Senior PGA Tour in 1990 and won two U.S. Senior Opens (1991 and 1993). By the close of the 20th century he won a total of 100 national and international tournaments, 18 of them major championships. He was one of only five professional golfers to win the Grand Slam (the others include Ben Hogan, Gary Player, Gene Sarazen, and Tiger Woods).

Careful in his preparation for a tournament, powerful and accurate in the play of his driver and long irons, and uncanny in his ability at making important putts, Nicklaus was considered the greatest final-round player ever. His career total of 18 major tournament victories became the standard by which all professional golfers are measured.

Called the Golden Bear for his sunlit blond hair and sturdy manner, Nicklaus used the nickname as the name of his company.

He wrote books on golf and designed more than 150 golf courses worldwide. From 1976 he hosted the Memorial Tournament on his Muirfield Village Golf Course in Ohio.

AL OERTER

(b. 1936–d. 2007)

Alfred Oerter was a discus thrower who won four consecutive Olympic gold medals (1956, 1960, 1964, and 1968), setting an Olympic record each time. During his career he set new world records four times (1962–64). He was the first to throw the discus more than 200 feet with his first world record of 61.10 meters (200 feet 5 inches). His best throw in setting a world record was 62.94 meters (206 feet 6 inches) in 1964; his best Olympic throw was 64.78 meters (212 feet 6 inches) in 1968.

Alfred Oerter, Jr. was born on September 19, 1936, in Astoria, Queens, New York. After taking up weight lifting in his teens to fill out his slender form, Oerter was a football player and sprinter in high school. He discovered his discus ability when he idly picked up the discus and threw it farther than anyone else on the track team could. He attended the University of Kansas on a track scholarship (1954–58) and won six national Amateur Athletic Union titles.

Although his original goal was to win five gold medals, Oerter retired from Olympic competition after the 1968 Games with four because of the sacrifices and pressures of being an Olympic champion. He resumed training in 1976, however. While he narrowly failed to qualify for the U.S. Olympic team in 1980, which ultimately did not compete (there being a U.S. boycott), he made the longest throw of his career and the world's longest that year, 69.46 meters (227 feet 11 inches). Though active at a world-class level into his 40s, he fell short again in bids for the U.S. Olympic team in 1984 and 1988. He was a world record holder in Masters track-and-field competition in the 1980s. Oerter was in the first class to be inducted into the U.S. Olympic Hall of Fame in 1983. He died on October 1, 2007, in Fort Myers, Florida.

SHAQUILLE O'NEAL

(b. 1972–)

As one of the most popular and highest-paid players in the National Basketball Association (NBA), Shaquille O'Neal overwhelmed the competition with his size and skills. A 7-foot-1-inch (2.16-meter) center who weighed at least 315 pounds (142.9 kilograms), "Shaq" was nevertheless an agile athlete. He was consistently one of the top players in the league in scoring and blocking. Along with teammate Kobe Bryant and coach Phil Jackson, O'Neal led the Los Angeles Lakers to three consecutive NBA championships (2000–02).

Shaquille Rashaun O'Neal was born on March 6, 1972, in Newark, New Jersey. His first name means "little one" in Arabic, and his middle name means "warrior." His father was a United States army sergeant, and military transfers caused Shaquille and his family to move frequently.

At age 13 O'Neal, already 6 feet 6 inches (1.98 meters) tall, met Louisiana State University (LSU) head basketball coach Dale Brown, who made an early pitch for O'Neal to join his team. In 1987 the family moved to San Antonio, Texas, where O'Neal's outstanding performance for his high school team launched an intense recruiting war among colleges and universities. O'Neal ultimately chose LSU, where his game improved enormously. Assisted by Brown and Hall of Fame centers Kareem Abdul-Jabbar and Bill Walton, O'Neal developed a combination of strength, speed, and agility that made him a challenging opponent and a hot prospect for the pros.

Against the wishes of his parents, O'Neal dropped out of school in April 1992 to become available for the upcoming NBA draft. Several months later, as the first draft pick, the 20-year-old center was signed by the Orlando Magic for a seven-year, $40 million contract, becoming the highest-paid rookie in the NBA. (O'Neal later completed his studies, earning a bachelor's degree from LSU in 2000.)

O'Neal went on to be chosen NBA Rookie of the Year and won all-rookie first team honors. That year O'Neal's record in scoring, rebounding, field-goal percentage, and blocked shots made him the only player in the league to finish in the top ten in all four categories. In one game O'Neal's dunk was so powerful he destroyed the hydraulic basket support system.

Although O'Neal was a top scorer, he struggled with free throws, normally scoring on only 50 to 60 percent of his shots. His opponents often resorted to a strategy known as "hack-a-Shaq"—intentionally fouling him before he could shoot a field goal and thus sending him to the free-throw line instead. O'Neal complained that he regularly took a beating on the court with officials calling only a fraction of the fouls committed against him.

After four years with the Magic, O'Neal was tempted by the Los Angeles Lakers in 1996 into signing a record-setting seven-year, $120 million contract. Although the Lakers' record improved with O'Neal as center, the team was unable to reach the NBA finals until after the 1999–2000 season, the first with Phil Jackson as head coach. Under Jackson, O'Neal developed into more of a team player, paying greater attention to his defense and rebounding.

In 2000 the Lakers won the NBA championship, and O'Neal was named the Most Valuable Player (MVP) of the regular season, the All-Star Game, and the NBA finals. The Lakers captured the NBA championship title again in 2001 and 2002. O'Neal was named the MVP of the finals for both years. The Lakers returned to NBA finals in 2004 but were defeated. Soon thereafter the team underwent major changes, chief among them a trade that sent O'Neal to the Miami Heat. O'Neal helped lead the Heat to its first NBA championship, in 2006.

In 1993 O'Neal wrote an autobiography with a coauthor. He later released rap CDs and appeared in the feature films *Blue Chips* (1994) and *Kazaam* (1996). In addition, O'Neal had multimillion-dollar endorsement contracts. In 2007 he starred in a reality television series in which he helped kids become physically fit.

In February 2008 O'Neal was traded to the Phoenix Suns. His playing style did not mix well with the Suns' up-tempo game, however, and despite having had a very solid 2008–09 season, he was traded to the Cleveland Cavaliers in June 2009. Following the completion of the 2009–10 season, O'Neal signed a two-year contract to play with the Boston Celtics but an Achilles tendon injury limited his play. O'Neal retired after the 2010–11 season. His career totals include 28,596 points (the seventh highest total in NBA history at the time of his retirement) and 15 All-Star game appearances.

BOBBY ORR

(b. 1948–)

Boston Bruins great Bobby Orr, on the ice during his rookie season as a pro, in 1966. Melchior DiGiacomo/Hulton Archive/Getty Images

Bobby Orr was a Canadian-American professional National Hockey League (NHL) ice hockey player, who was the first defenseman to lead the NHL in scoring.

Robert Gordon Orr was born on March 20, 1948, in Parry Sound, Ontario, Canada. He came to the attention of Boston Bruin scouts when he was 12, and he was signed to a junior amateur contract. He joined the Bruins in 1966, when he had reached the legally required age of 18, and played with them for 10 seasons, during which time he helped the Bruins to the play-offs eight consecutive seasons and to two Stanley cups.

Orr was a highly decorated player and received more than 16 major awards in his career, including the Norris Trophy as most valuable defenseman (1967–75). In the 1968–69 season he scored 21 goals and made 43 assists (64 points) for a season record for a defenseman. In his career he set seasonal defenseman records for goals (46), assists (102), and points (139). He won the Art Ross Trophy for most points scored (1970 and 1975) and the Hart Trophy for most valuable player (1970–72).

Orr was frequently injured in the course of play. He was traded to the Chicago Black Hawks in 1976, where he served as assistant coach during the 1976–77 season. He retired in 1979, the same year of his induction into the Hockey Hall of Fame. After his retirement as a player, Orr received the Lester Patrick Trophy for outstanding contributions to hockey in the United States.

JESSE OWENS

(b. 1913–d. 1980)

Jesse Owens, crossing the finish line during a track and field event at the 1936 Olympics in Berlin. Owens won four gold medals at the Olympiad. Central Press/ Hulton Archive/Getty Images

The Olympic Games of 1936 were held in Berlin, Germany, under the new Nazi regime. It was Adolf Hitler's intent to use the games to demonstrate what he believed to be the superiority of the Aryan, or white, race. This aim was seriously weakened when Jesse Owens, an African American, won four gold medals in track and field events.

James Cleveland Owens was born in Oakville, Alabama, on September 12, 1913. In the early 1920s, Owens's family moved to Cleveland, Ohio, in search of better economic and educational opportunities. He set his first track records in the high jump and the running broad jump while a pupil at Fairmount Junior High School in 1928. Jesse became a track star in high school, and at the end of his senior year, he broke three national interscholastic records at the national scholastic meet in Chicago. He enrolled at Ohio

State University in September 1933 and had a remarkable track career there.

On one day—May 25, 1935—during a Big Ten meet at the University of Michigan, Owens equaled the world record for the 100-yard dash (9.4 seconds) and set new world records for the 220-yard dash (20.3 seconds), the 220-yard low hurdles (22.6 seconds), and the running broad jump (26 feet 8 1/4 inches, or 8.13 meters). In Berlin, Owens set a broad jump record that lasted for 25 years. He also tied the Olympic record for the 100-meter run (10.3 seconds) and set a new world record in the 200-meter race (20.7 seconds).

After his Olympic triumph, Owens graduated in 1937 and worked for a number of years for the Illinois Athletic Commission. He left the commission in 1955 and made goodwill trips to India and the Far East for the State Department. Owens died in Phoenix, Arizona, on March 31, 1980.

SATCHEL PAIGE

(b. 1906?–d. 1982)

Often referred to as one of the best pitchers in the history of baseball, Satchel Paige combined pinpoint accuracy with high velocity to make himself the most effective pitcher of his era. He also is recognized as one of the first group of players to make the jump from the Negro Leagues to the major leagues.

Leroy Robert Paige was born in Mobile, Alabama. The precise date is unknown, and Paige himself would never confirm his actual age. One of 12 children, Paige rarely attended school and often found himself in trouble with authority figures. Paige worked at a train station carrying luggage for tips as a boy and once tried to make off with the satchel of a passenger. The man chased him down and recovered the bag, but a friend witnessed the incident and nicknamed him Satchel. The nickname would stick with Paige for the rest of his life, though he often told various fictitious stories about how he got it.

Paige eventually found himself in reform school, where he discovered baseball. There he learned to be a pitcher and worked hard at polishing his game. After leaving the school, Paige played on various semiprofessional teams for the next two years. In 1926, Paige broke into the professional ranks when he was picked up by Chattanooga of the Negro Southern League. His first professional campaign was uneventful as Paige received few opportunities to pitch. While he always threw with great velocity, the pinpoint control for which he became famous was absent during that first season, and Paige struggled with wild pitches.

Prior to the 1927 season, Paige moved to the Negro National League's Birmingham Black Barons, where he became a regular pitcher for the first time at the professional level. Paige moved from one team to another during the 1930s and 1940s, always searching for an owner who would offer a more lucrative contract. He is probably best remembered for his contributions to the great Pittsburgh Crawfords teams of the early 1930s and for leading the Kansas City Monarchs to four consecutive championships, from 1939 to 1942. As an individual, Paige's best years were in the early 1930s, when he had seasons of 32 and 31 victories in 1932 and 1933 and 24 wins in 1936. In 1935 he pitched 153 games, starting 29 times in one month. During the Monarchs' sweep of the Homestead (Pa.) Grays in the 1942 World Series, Paige collected three victories in the series. He was also selected to pitch in the annual East-West All-Star game five times.

In 1948, Paige achieved a dream as Bill Veeck of the Cleveland Indians signed him on, in the process making Paige the major leagues' oldest rookie. In his first season with the Indians, Paige recorded a 6–1 record and posted a 2.48 earned run average while helping lead the team to a world championship. In 1951 he joined the St. Louis Browns and went on to consecutive all-star game appearances in 1952 and 1953. Paige made history once again in 1965 when, at the alleged age of 59, he pitched three innings for the Kansas City Athletics, making him the oldest player in major league history.

The stories and folklore surrounding Paige's career are as important to understanding Paige as are his impressive statistics. Paige often guaranteed he would strike out the first nine hitters that he faced and he usually followed through on this boast. He was legendary for calling in his outfielders to sit behind the pitcher's mound and watch as he proceeded to strike out the other side with the tying run on base. He often warmed up before games by throwing 20 pitches across a tiny home plate, usually a gum wrapper. Comments from opposing hitters—for example, that Paige's fastball looked as small as a pea when it reached home plate—embellished his always-growing legend.

Paige was the best pitcher of his era and is recognized as one of the best, if not the best, of all time. His career in professional baseball spanned more than three decades in which he piled up many individual achievements and was a part of several championship teams. In the crowning moment of his career, Satchel Paige became the first player from the Negro Leagues to be inducted into the National Baseball Hall of Fame, in 1971. He died on June 8, 1982, in Kansas City, Missouri.

ARNOLD PALMER

(b. 1929–)

Arnold Palmer was the first professional golfer to earn more than a million dollars a year in prize money, the first golfer to fly his own plane to tournaments, and the first to win the Masters four times—in 1958, 1960, 1962, and 1964. From 1954, when he became a professional, through 1975 he won 61 tournaments sanctioned by the Professional Golfers' Association of America (PGA). Whenever Palmer appeared on a golf course, his many fans—dubbed "Arnie's Army"—were sure to follow.

Arnold Palmer was born in Youngstown, Penn., on September 10, 1929. His father was a golf professional at the Latrobe Country Club. Arnold was given cut-down clubs at the age of 3, and his father taught him a firm grip. By the time he entered high school he was already an excellent golfer. Palmer attended Wake Forest University on a golf scholarship from 1947 until 1954, with time out for service in the United States Coast Guard. He left college without a degree and worked briefly as a salesman. Palmer turned professional in 1954 after winning the

United States Amateur championship. The next year he won his first professional tournament, the Canadian Open. In addition to his four Masters Tournament victories, Palmer won the United States Open in 1960 and the British Open in 1961 and 1962. His total winnings were more than a million dollars by 1967. In 1970 Palmer was named athlete of the decade.

By the late 1960s Palmer was gradually overtaken in PGA tour victories by a younger golfer named Jack Nicklaus. By the late 1970s Palmer was playing in professional golf's senior circuit. He won senior tournaments in 1980, 1981, and 1984. Much of his time was devoted to Arnold Palmer Enterprises, a division of the National Broadcasting Company. In 1982 he negotiated an agreement to build the first golf course in China.

WALTER PAYTON

(b. 1954–d. 1999)

Walter Jerry Payton was born in Columbia, Mississippi, on July 25, 1954. Known as "Sweetness," Payton was considered by many coaches and players to be the best all-around back to play the game. Before his retirement, at the end of the 1987 season, Payton gained 16,726 yards, bettering the previous record by more than 4,400 yards.

Besides being football's all-time leading rusher, Payton was a capable blocker, pass receiver, and even passer. He was best known, however, for his ability to escape tacklers, be it by "high-stepping," "stiff-arming," or literally leaping over them. On October 7, 1984, as Chicago Bears running back, Payton broke Jim Brown's National Football League (NFL) record for the most yards gained in a career.

His severe training regimen was the envy of athletes in and out of professional football, which contributed to his extraordinary toughness. Payton started in more than 180 consecutive games in his career.

He did not play football until he was a junior at Columbia High School. During his college career at Jackson State University in Jackson, Miss., he set a National Collegiate Athletic Association record for most points scored. He received a bachelor's degree in special education in 1975. The Chicago Bears of the NFL selected him on the fourth pick in the first round of the 1975 draft.

Some of his many NFL records include 3,838 rushing attempts; 21,803 yards combined rushing, receiving, and return; 275 yards rushing in a single game; 77 games rushing 100 yards or more; ten 1,000-yard seasons; 110 rushing touchdowns; and three consecutive combined 2,000-yard seasons. He was in nine Pro Bowl games and was a star of the 1985 Bears Super Bowl season. His last home game was on January 10, 1988, during the play-offs. He was elected to the Pro Football Hall of Fame in January 1993, in his first year of eligibility. During his final year of life, while suffering from a rare liver disease, Payton was credited with reviving national interest in organ donation. He died at his home in Barrington, Illinois, on November 1, 1999.

PELÉ

(b. 1940–)

Soccer (association football) superstar Pelé was the world's most famous and highest-paid athlete when he joined a North American team in 1975. He led the Brazilian national soccer team to three World Cup victories in 1958, 1962, and 1970, and to permanent possession of the Jules Rimet Trophy.

Edson Arantes do Nascimento (Pelé) was born to a poor family on Oct. 23, 1940, in Três Corações, Brazil. He began playing for a local minor-league club when he was a teenager. He made his debut with the Santos Football Club in 1956. With Pelé at inside left forward, the team won several South American clubs' cups and the 1962 world club championship, in addition to the three World Cup championships.

Pelé scored his 1,000th goal in 1969. The legendary athlete retired in 1974 but made a comeback in 1975 after accepting a reported $7-million contract for three years with the New York Cosmos of the North American Soccer League. He said he came out of retirement, not for the money, but to "make soccer truly popular in the

Soccer legend Pelé (foreground), playing in a non-tournament "friendly" match against Malmoe FF in Sweden, 1960. AFP/Getty Images

United States." His farewell appearance was against his old Santos club in 1977.

Pelé, whose nickname does not mean anything, became a Brazilian national hero and was also known as Pérola Negra ("Black Pearl"). An average-sized man, he was blessed with speed, great balance, amazing vision, the ability to control the ball superbly, and the ability to shoot powerfully and accurately with either foot and with his head. In his career he played in 1,363 matches and scored 1,281 goals. His best season was 1958, when he scored 139 times.

In addition to his accomplishments in sports, he published several best-selling autobiographies, starred in several documentary and semi-documentary films, and composed numerous musical pieces, including the entire sound track for the film *Pelé* (1977). He was the

1978 recipient of the International Peace Award, and in 1980 he was named athlete of the century.

MICHAEL PHELPS

(b. 1985–)

Michael Phelps was born on June 30, 1985, in Baltimore, Maryland. Phelps is the most decorated athlete in the history of the Olympic Games. He won a total of 22 Olympic medals, 18 of them gold.

His older sisters, Whitney and Hilary, were competitive swimmers, and Phelps spent his early years accompanying them to practices and competitions. He joined the prestigious North Baltimore Aquatic Club at the age of seven. In 1996 he began training under coach Bob Bowman, who would remain Phelps's personal coach throughout the swimmer's career.

In 2000 Phelps qualified for the U.S. Olympic team, placing second at the trials in the 200-meter butterfly and went on to finish fifth in the event at the Olympic Games in Sydney, Australia. At the 2001 U.S. spring nationals he became, at age 15, the youngest world-record holder in the history of men's swimming when he posted a time of 1 minute, 54.92 seconds in the 200-meter butterfly. At the world championships in Fukuoka, Japan, that year, he won his first international title. He won five medals, three of them gold, at the 2002 Pan Pacific championships. The next year at the U.S. spring nationals, he became the first male swimmer to earn titles in three different strokes at a single national championship, and he later broke an unprecedented five individual world records at the world championships in Barcelona, Spain. Phelps also captured five titles at the U.S. summer nationals—the most won by a male swimmer at a single championship. He won the James E. Sullivan Award in 2003 as the top amateur athlete in the United States.

At the 2004 Olympic Games in Athens, Greece, Phelps's medal tally included gold in the 200-meter and 400-meter individual medley (IM) events, the 100-meter and 200-meter butterfly, the 4 × 200-meter freestyle relay, and the 4 × 100-meter medley relay; he took bronze in the 200-meter freestyle and the 4 × 100-meter freestyle relay. Phelps set five world or Olympic records in Athens, and his four individual swimming gold medals tied a record set by American Mark Spitz at the 1972 Games in Munich, West Germany (now in Germany). Phelps also won seven gold medals at the 2007 world championships in Melbourne, Australia. Phelps tied Spitz for most wins at a major international meet, with his seven titles.

Phelps entered the 2008 Olympic Games in Beijing, China, with the goal of breaking Spitz's record of seven gold medals at one Olympics. He surpassed Spitz's mark by winning in five individual events and three relays. Phelps set world records in the 400-meter IM, the 200-meter freestyle, the 200-meter butterfly, and the 200-meter IM, and he set an Olympic record in the 100-meter butterfly. In addition, Phelps helped lead the U.S. men to new world marks in the 4 × 100-meter freestyle relay, the 4 × 200-meter freestyle relay, and the 4 × 100-meter medley relay.

At the 2009 world championships in Rome, Italy, Phelps won five golds (100-meter and 200-meter butterfly, 4 × 100-meter and 4 × 200-meter freestyle relay, and 4 × 100-meter medley relay) and a silver (200-meter freestyle). He continued his string of medal-winning performances at the 2011 world championships in Shanghai, China, where he claimed four golds (100- and 200-meter butterfly, 4 × 100-meter medley relay, and 4 × 200-meter freestyle relay), two silvers (200-meter freestyle and 200-meter IM), and one bronze (4 × 100-meter freestyle relay).

At the 2012 Olympics in London, England, Phelps failed to medal in his first event, the 400-meter IM, but he subsequently won silver medals in both the 4 × 100-meter freestyle relay and 200-meter butterfly and a gold medal in the 4 × 200-meter freestyle relay. With the latter win, he captured his 19th career Olympic medal, surpassing the record set by Soviet gymnast Larisa Latynina. Before the swimming competition was over in London, Phelps added three more gold medals to his collection (200-meter IM, 100-meter butterfly, and 4 × 100-meter medley relay). With his victory in the 200-meter IM, in which he narrowly bested his longtime rival, fellow American Ryan Lochte, Phelps became the first male swimmer to win the same individual event at three consecutive Olympics. His later victory in the 100-meter butterfly also marked the third consecutive time he had won gold in that event.

ALBERT PUJOLS

(b. 1980–)

First baseman Albert Pujols ranks among a select group of baseball players who hit consistently for both average and power. Even early in his career, he was already considered to be one of the game's all-time greatest hitters.

José Alberto Pujols Alcántara was born on Jan. 16, 1980, in Santo Domingo, the capital of the Dominican Republic. The Pujols family immigrated to the United States when Albert was 16, and they eventually settled in Missouri. Pujols impressed major league scouts with his play at both the high school and collegiate level, and he was selected by the St. Louis Cardinals in the 1999 draft. In 2001 he earned a spot on the Cardinals' roster.

Presumed to be a reserve as he entered his first season, Pujols instead played his way into the starting lineup. He posted a .329 batting average with 37 home runs and 130 runs batted in (RBI), and he was the unanimous choice for 2001 National League (NL) rookie of the year. Pujols continued to put up impressive offensive numbers in the following seasons and collected a number of awards, including the 2004 NL Championship Series Most Valuable Player (MVP) and Silver Slugger awards in 2001, 2003, and 2004. In 2005 he hit .330 with 41 home runs and 117 RBI and was named NL MVP.

In 2006 Pujols bettered the batting statistics of his previous season, hitting .331 with 49 home runs and 137 RBI. That year he also helped lead St. Louis to a World Series title. In 2008 Pujols was again named NL MVP after finishing the season with a .357 batting average and 116 RBI. The following year he won his third NL MVP award after hitting .327 with 47 home runs and 135 RBI.

JERRY RICE

(b. 1962–)

M any consider Rice to be the greatest wide receiver in the history of the National Football League (NFL). Playing primarily for the San Francisco 49ers, he set a host of NFL records, including those for career touchdowns (208), receptions (1,549), and reception yardage (22,895).

Jerry Lee Rice was born on October 13, 1962, in Starkville, Mississippi. Rice attended Mississippi Valley State University in Itta Bena on a football scholarship. There he earned All-America honors and set 18 records in Division I-AA of the National Collegiate Athletic Association, including most catches in a single game (24).

Rice was drafted by the San Francisco 49ers in the first round of the 1985 NFL draft. He struggled at first, but in his second season he caught 86 passes and led the league in reception yardage (1,570) and touchdown receptions (15). Rice prospered in San Francisco's so-called West Coast offense, which relied on many short, quick passes by the quarterback and accurate route running by the receivers. He set a single-season record for touchdown receptions (22) in 1987, even though a players' strike limited the season to 12 games, and was named NFL player of the year. Led by Rice and quarterback Joe Montana, the 49ers won the Super Bowl at the end of the 1988, 1989, and 1994 seasons. Rice was named the Most Valuable Player of Super Bowl XXIII (1988 season), and he set many Super Bowl records. He was named to the annual Pro Bowl from 1986 through 1998.

In a controversial move to develop younger players, the 49ers traded Rice to the Oakland Raiders before the 2001 season. The following season he became the first player to score more than 200 career touchdowns as he helped the Raiders reach Super Bowl XXXVII, where they were defeated by the Tampa Bay Buccaneers. In 2003 he made his 13th Pro Bowl appearance. Midway through the

2004 season, Rice was traded to the Seattle Seahawks, but he was released by the team at the end of the season. After an unsuccessful attempt to become a starting receiver for the Denver Broncos the following year, he signed a ceremonial one-day contract with San Francisco and retired as a 49er. Rice was inducted into the Pro Football Hall of Fame in 2010.

CAL RIPKEN, JR.

(b. 1960–)

While many fans of professional sports were sad about the greed and indifference that seemed to describe most modern players, Cal Ripken, Jr., emerged as one of baseball's most heroic athletes. On Sept. 6, 1995, the polite shortstop for the Baltimore Orioles played his 2,131st consecutive game, surpassing Lou Gehrig's so-called Iron Man record, which had stood for more than 56 years. Ripken spent his entire career in Baltimore, retiring in 2001 with 3,184 hits, 1,695 runs batted in (RBIs), 431 home runs, and a lifetime batting average of .276.

Calvin Edwin Ripken, Jr., was born on Aug. 24, 1960, in Havre de Grace, Maryland. His father, Cal Ripken, Sr., was a minor league manager and later a coach for the Orioles. When Ripken, Jr., was in high school, he took batting practice at the Orioles' stadium and peppered the outfield seats with baseballs. His father was impressed with the boy's strength and bat speed and suspected that his son had a chance for major league stardom. The baseball talent scouts agreed when, during his senior year of high school, Ripken batted .492 with 29 RBIs in 20 games. As a pitcher, he achieved a 7-2 won-lost record, a 0.70 earned-run average, and 100 strikeouts in 60 innings.

The Orioles drafted Ripken and sent him to their minor league system, where he made all-league teams in three consecutive minor-league seasons. The Orioles traded third baseman Doug DeCinces to make room for Ripken in their 1982 lineup. Ripken finished the season with 28 home runs and 93 RBIs and was named American League Rookie of the Year. During the season he switched from playing third base to the shortstop position because the Orioles had a more urgent need there.

Ripken's consecutive-game streak began on May 30, 1982. He did not play every inning of every game during his streak (he was ejected during the first inning on two separate occasions). From June 5, 1982, to Sept. 14, 1987, however, he played 8,243 consecutive innings. His streak ended on Sept. 20, 1998, when he voluntarily took himself out of the lineup for the last home game of the 1998 season. He had played in 2,632 consecutive games.

Ripken led the Orioles to a World Series title in 1983. That same year, he was named the American League's Most Valuable Player (MVP) after leading the majors in hits with 211 and posting a .318 batting average. He received MVP honors again in 1991, when he batted .323 and tallied 210 hits.

Ripken won Gold Glove awards for fielding excellence in 1991 and 1992. He played in 19 All-Star Games during his career, making his last appearance in 2001, when he was chosen as the game's MVP. Ripken was elected to the Baseball Hall of Fame in 2007.

JACKIE ROBINSON
(b. 1919–d. 1972)

Jackie Robinson was the first African American athlete to play in baseball's major leagues in the 20th century. By breaking the color barrier in 1947, Robinson made great progress not only for black athletes but also for all concerned with racial justice.

Jack Roosevelt Robinson was born on Jan. 31, 1919, in Cairo, Georgia, but grew up in Pasadena, California. After showing remarkable athletic ability during high school and junior college, he excelled at baseball, football, basketball, and track at the University of California at Los Angeles (UCLA) and became the first student at the school to earn four letters in one year. He left UCLA in 1941 and briefly played professional football before being drafted into the United States Army. During his service, he refused to sit at the back of a bus and was threatened with a

Jackie Robinson, posing for a player portrait in the 1940s. Hulton Archive/
Getty Images

court-martial, but the charges were dropped and he was given an honorable discharge in 1945.

While playing baseball for the Kansas City Monarchs in the Negro National League, Robinson caught the eye of a scout for the Brooklyn (now Los Angeles) Dodgers and was brought to the attention of team president Branch Rickey. Major league baseball was closed to black players at the time. Rickey thought that this was wrong, and he wanted to find someone who could successfully integrate the sport. After meeting Robinson and being impressed with his courage as well as his skill, Rickey signed him on October 23, 1945, to play for the Dodgers' AAA team in Montreal. During the 1946 season, Robinson batted .349 with the farm club and led the team to victory in the Little World Series.

While playing baseball for the Kansas City Monarchs in the Negro National League, Robinson made his major league debut in April 1947. The chief problem he had to overcome was controlling his temper in the face of continual racial slurs from the crowds and other ballplayers, including some of his own teammates. Robinson did not break his promise to Rickey to remain silent, though pitchers sometimes deliberately threw at him, hotels at away games often would not accommodate him, and he and his family received death threats. He instead let his actions do the talking by batting .297 and leading the National League in stolen bases. He was chosen Rookie of the Year at season's end.

Robinson's .342 average made him the league's batting champion and most valuable player in 1949. During his career, which he spent primarily as a second baseman, Robinson helped the Dodgers capture six National League pennants and one World Series title. He retired in 1956 with a .311 lifetime batting average and 197 total stolen bases. The Dodgers later retired his number 42 jersey. When he was elected to the Baseball Hall of Fame in 1962 he was the first black player to be honored.

After he left baseball Robinson pursued business interests while continuing to work on behalf of civil rights. Diabetes and heart problems plagued his later life, and he died on Oct. 24, 1972, in Stamford, Conn. His wife established the Jackie Robinson Foundation the following year to provide minority scholarships. In 1997, major league baseball held a season-long celebration marking the 50th anniversary of his historic debut.

Robinson's tombstone reads "A life is not important except in the impact it has on other lives."

RONALDO

(b. 1976–)

R onaldo's awesome presence and almost unstoppable skills earned him an international reputation as one of soccer's most talented young players in the 1990s. Displaying a boyish joy for the sport, Ronaldo possessed strength, speed, and well-practiced skill. In 1996 Ronaldo became the youngest soccer player ever to receive the World Player of the Year award.

Ronaldo Luis Nazário de Lima was born on Sept. 22, 1976, in Itaguai, Brazil, and grew up in Bento Ribeiro, a poor suburb of Rio de Janeiro. He began playing soccer as a junior for the neighborhood Social Ramos Club at age 12 and two years later joined São Cristóvão, a smaller club in the city. When he was 15 years old Ronaldo made his professional debut as a forward with the team Cruzeiro in the city of Belo Horizonte, north of Rio de Janeiro. Ronaldo scored 58 goals in 60 games for the club. He then moved to Europe to play for the Dutch club PSV Eindhoven. Scoring 55 goals in 56 games over two seasons, Ronaldo was sold to Spanish club Barcelona in 1996. During his single season with Barcelona he made 34 goals in 37 games and led the team to victory at the European Cup–Winners' Cup before transferring to the Italian club Internazionale of Milan. Ronaldo finished the 1997–98 season as the second-leading scorer in Italy's Series A league, with 25 goals in 32 matches.

Ronaldo made his Brazilian national team debut in March 1994. At the 1994 World Cup, 17-year-old Ronaldo, the youngest player on Brazil's squad, watched from the sidelines as his country's team won the championship. Two years later, Ronaldo played an active role in Brazil's bronze-medal win at the 1996 Olympic Games. He led Brazil to victory at the 1997 Copa América against Bolivia.

Ronaldo was only 20 years old when he was honored as the 1996 World Player of the Year. In 1997 the Fédération Internationale de Football Association (FIFA), soccer's international governing body, again named Ronaldo World Player of the Year, marking the first time a player was awarded the title in two consecutive years. Ronaldo was also recognized as the European Player of the Year for the 1996–97 season.

In 1999 Ronaldo suffered a serious knee injury that left him unable to play for almost two years. He returned to competitive play in 2001. At the 2002 World Cup in Japan he scored eight goals to earn the Golden Boot award as the tournament's top scorer and helped Brazil win its fifth World Cup championship. That year he was also named the World Player of the Year for the third time in his career as well as the European Player of the Year. He then joined Real Madrid of Spain.

At the 2006 World Cup Ronaldo scored three goals to bring his career total at the tournament to a record-setting 15. While playing for Italy's AC Milan in 2008, he ruptured a tendon in his left knee—the same type of injury that had occurred in his right knee in 1999. In December 2008 a fully recovered Ronaldo signed with the Corinthians in São Paulo. However, he continued to be troubled by a number of other, less significant, leg injuries during his time with the Corinthians. Ronaldo then suffered a thyroid condition that made him gain weight, and he abruptly retired from the sport in February 2011.

CRISTIANO RONALDO

(b. 1985–)

Cristiano Ronaldo was considered by many to be the most gifted soccer (association football) player of his generation. Among the awards and honors he has received, Ronaldo was voted the Fédération Internationale de Football Association (FIFA) World Player of the Year for 2008.

Cristiano Ronaldo was born on February 5, 1985, in Funchal, Portugal, and started playing soccer when he was 9 years old. He debuted on Sporting Clube de Portugal's first team in 2002 and signed with Manchester United the following year, becoming the first Portuguese to join the celebrated British squad.

Ronaldo was an instant wonder with United and soon came to be regarded as one of the best forwards in the game. His finest season with the team came in 2007–08, when he earned the Golden Shoe award as

Real Madrid's Cristiano Ronaldo, shown in action during a 2012 La Liga match in Madrid. Denis Doyle/Getty Images

Europe's leading scorer. He led United to a Champions League title in May 2008 and powered the team's run to the 2009 Champions League final, which they lost to FC Barcelona.

In addition to his success with United, Ronaldo was a key player in the Portuguese national team since his debut in August 2003. Portugal was the host of the 2004 European Championship, during which Ronaldo scored two goals and helped his side reach the final against Greece. But Ronaldo and Portugal failed to score against the Greeks and lost 1–0. Two years later, Portugal proved to be one of the most spectacular teams in the 2006 World Cup, with Ronaldo helping the squad to a fourth-place finish.

In the spring of 2009, the soccer world was shaken when Spanish team Real Madrid announced that Ronaldo was leaving Manchester United to join the Spanish powerhouse for a record-breaking transfer of $132 million. The transfer made Ronaldo the most expensive player in soccer history.

WILMA RUDOLPH

(b. 1940–d. 1994)

Nobody who knew Wilma Rudolph during her childhood ever would have guessed that she would grow up to be a track and field superstar. A series of illnesses early in life left Rudolph without the use of one leg, and only constant exercise and care enabled her finally to walk when she was eight. However, she went on to excel at sports in high school and college, and in 1960 she became the first American woman runner to win three gold medals at a single Olympics.

Wilma Glodean Rudolph was born prematurely on June 23, 1940, in St. Bethlehem, Tennessee. She was the 20th of 22 children her father had between two marriages. She spent most of her childhood in bed— suffering from pneumonia, scarlet fever, and polio. She hated the metal leg braces she needed to wear and longed to move about like other kids. With her family's help in massaging her crippled leg and driving her to physical therapy, Rudolph traded her braces for special shoes. She was later able to get rid of those, too.

During high school Rudolph became a star basketball player and runner. At the age of 14, she attracted the attention of a track coach from Tennessee State University, at Nashville, the school from which she later graduated in 1963. She worked with him during summers to improve her sprinting skills. At the age of 16, Rudolph traveled to Melbourne, Australia, for the 1956 Summer Olympics and received a bronze medal as a member of the 4 × 100-meter relay team.

Rudolph was the Amateur Athletic Union (AAU) 100-yard-dash champion from 1959 to 1962. In 1960, before the Olympic Games at Rome, she set a world record of 22.9 seconds for the 200-meter race. In the Games themselves she won gold medals in the 100-meter dash (tying the world record of 11.3 seconds in the semifinals), the 200-meter dash (running the opening heat in 23.2 seconds to break the Olympic record), and the 4 x 100-meter relay (anchoring the team to a new world record of 44.4 seconds in a semifinal race). The AAU presented Rudolph with its Sullivan Award in 1961 as the year's outstanding amateur athlete.

Feeling that she might not be able to achieve the same level of success, Rudolph refused to participate in the 1964 Olympics. After retiring as a runner, Rudolph taught, coached, gave motivational speeches, and became a mother. She worked on Operation Champion to provide children and teenagers in the nation's largest ghettos with sports training from star athletes. She also founded the Wilma Rudolph Foundation to promote amateur athletics and to encourage children to overcome obstacles.

Rudolph was named to the National Track and Field Hall of Fame in 1974, the International Sports Hall of Fame in 1980, and the U.S. Olympic Hall of Fame in 1983. Her autobiography, *Wilma*, was published in 1977 and was made into a television movie that same year. Rudolph died from brain cancer on Nov. 12, 1994, in Brentwood, Tenn.

BABE RUTH

(b. 1895–d. 1948)

The crowd that jammed Chicago's Wrigley Field booed when the big man with the barrel-shaped body and pipe-stem legs came up to bat. It was the third game of the 1932 World Series between the Chicago Cubs and the New York Yankees. The score was 4–4 in the fifth inning. Cub pitcher Charlie Root threw one strike, then another. Grinning, the batter stepped back and seemed to point to the distant center-field bleachers. Root pitched, the big man swung, and the ball soared into the bleachers for a home run. The hitter was Babe Ruth, probably the most worshipped of baseball players. Ruth's legendary pointing gesture—whether it ever happened or whether he even intended it—captured the imagination of baseball fans, as did everything about this great player.

George Herman Ruth was born in Baltimore, Maryland, on February 6, 1895. The Babe's achievements loom large in the record books. The left-hander held or shared about 60 records, with 28 made in World Series games. Among them was his record of pitching 29 consecutive scoreless innings in World Series play and his total of 714 major league homers—not including 15 World Series homers. (The pitching and home-run records were later broken by Whitey Ford and Hank Aaron.)

His father, a saloonkeeper, placed him in St. Mary's Industrial School when George was 7. There he learned to play baseball. In 1914, through the help of one of the priests who taught at the school, Ruth began to play with the Baltimore Orioles of the International League. The Orioles' manager, Jack Dunn, paid him $600 for his first season. Although Ruth later earned such nicknames as the Sultan of Swat and the Busting Bambino, he got his most famous nickname—Babe—on his first day of practice. A veteran coach sneered at the 6-foot-2 youngster, "Here's another one of Dunn's babes."

Later in the season he was sold to the Boston Red Sox. As his batting prowess grew, he was shifted from the pitcher's mound to the outfield, where he could play every day. Before he quit pitching, Ruth had won 94 games and lost 46.

In 1920 Ruth was sold for $125,000 to the New York Yankees, whose stadium was later called the House That Ruth Built. Thus began the greatest years of his career. He reached his peak in 1927, when he hit 60 home runs, a season record (for 154 games) that still stands. In 1925 he was suspended for "misconduct" off the field. As Ruth grew older, his huge body became too heavy for his slender legs. In 1935, after 15 years with the Yankees, he joined the Boston Braves as a playing vice president. Before the season ended, the unhappy Ruth laid down his bat for the last time. He ended his career in baseball

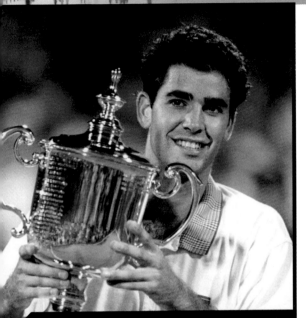

Pete Sampras, holding the winner's trophy at the U.S. Open in 1996. It was Sampras's fourth of five U.S. Open wins, and just one of his 14 Grand Slam titles. Shaun Botterill/Hulton Archive/ Getty Images

as a coach for the Brooklyn Dodgers in 1938.

In 1947 Ruth, who had always loved children, took a position with the Ford Motor Company to help with its Legion junior baseball program. He died of throat cancer in New York City on Aug. 16, 1948, with one dream unfulfilled: his reputation for irresponsibility blocked his wish to manage a big-league team.

PETE SAMPRAS

(b. 1971–)

Pete Sampras had one of the fastest serves in the game. He held the record for winning the most men's Grand Slam singles championships ever—14 in total, with seven at Wimbledon, five at the U.S. Open, and two at the Australian Open. His record among male players stood until 2009 when it was broken by Roger Federer.

Sampras was born in Washington, D.C., on August 12, 1971. When he was seven years old the family moved to Palos Verdes, California, where Sampras and his sister Stella played tennis on public courts. As their talent became obvious, the family joined a club and engaged a coach, Peter Fischer. Stella would eventually win the women's national collegiate doubles title and become head coach at the University of California at Los Angeles. Pete knew by age 12 that he wanted to play tennis professionally. He watched videotapes of his idol, Australian star Rod Laver. He played in junior tournaments, usually ranking among the top 25 boys in the United States, and he made the Boys' Junior Davis Cup team in 1987.

Sampras left high school after his junior year to turn professional in 1988. His first two years of professional tennis were undistinguished. By early 1990 he had a new coach and had moved to Florida. Sampras played at Wimbledon that summer but was eliminated in the first round.

Sampras's first Grand Slam title made him a celebrity in September 1990, when he became the youngest man ever to win the U.S. Open. The clean-cut and quiet 6-foot 1-inch (1.85-meter) champion made many public appearances, including playing doubles with President George Bush at the White House.

Sampras did not win another Grand Slam event for nearly three years. Some people accused him of not trying, others blamed injuries and bad luck. He won the November 1991 Association of Tennis Professionals (ATP) world championship and helped win the 1992 Davis Cup. By April 1993 lesser victories raised his rank to number one, but some questioned whether he deserved it.

That changed with Sampras's victory at Wimbledon in July 1993. He went on to win his second U.S. Open in 1993, followed by the Australian Open and Wimbledon in 1994. He retained the number one ranking throughout 1994, despite suffering from ankle injuries toward the end of the year.

Sampras's friend and coach Tim Gullikson was diagnosed with cancer in 1995 and died in 1996. Sampras was deeply affected. He won Wimbledon and the U.S. Open in 1995 but lost the ATP title and the next three Grand Slam events.

Sampras bounced back in the second half of 1996 to win his fourth U.S. Open title and his third ATP world championship. He won the Australian Open in January 1997 and Wimbledon in July 1997. Sampras won at Wimbledon again in 1998, and he ranked number one in the world for a record sixth consecutive year. He captured the Wimbledon title again the following year. When Sampras defeated Patrick Rafter in 2000 to win his seventh Wimbledon championship, he not only beat Roy Emerson's Grand Slam record, but also tied the record for most All-England Club wins set by William Renshaw in 1889.

Sampras did not win any ATP tournaments during the next two years, leading some to question whether he should retire. He triumphed at the 2002 U.S. Open, however, defeating Andre Agassi in the finals to win his 14th Grand Slam championship, at age 31. In 2003 Sampras officially retired from professional tennis. He was inducted into the International Tennis Hall of Fame in 2007.

BARRY SANDERS

(b. 1968–)

B arry Sanders became the third player in NFL history to rush for 2,000 yards in a single season. He achieved this at the end of the 1997–98 season. He was the only professional football player to start his career in professional football with eight consecutive seasons of rushing at least 1,000 yards.

Barry Sanders was born on July 16, 1968, in Wichita, Kansas, the seventh of eleven children of William Sanders, a self-employed construction worker, and his wife, Shirley. Since turning professional in 1989 after his junior year in college, Sanders stacked up numerous NFL rushing records with his exceptional ability to move laterally at full speed. His speed, and reflexes that allowed him to dodge seemingly unavoidable hits, protected him from injuries during his astonishing NFL career.

Sanders had a stern but loving father who encouraged his sons to work hard in school as well as in sports to keep them out of trouble. Shirley Sanders, a quiet, religious woman, was active in the Baptist church. Sanders was also influenced by his oldest brother, who had a troubled youth but later became a minister.

Although Sanders loved basketball, his ability to stop abruptly and move quickly from side to side, were skills that launched his football career in high school. At 5 feet, 8 inches (1.7 meters) tall, he was considered small in comparison to other players and was relegated to the position of defensive back. When he finally got the opportunity to start as tailback, he demonstrated the flashes of greatness that would propel him into football history.

Sanders had wanted to play for the University of Oklahoma but ended up at the smaller Oklahoma State University because it had a better business program. After breaking records for several years—and increasing his weight from 175 pounds to 200 pounds (80 to 90 kilograms)—Sanders ended up the 1988–89 National Collegiate Athletic Association (NCAA) season with the prestigious Heisman Trophy. Shortly thereafter, he was chosen by the Detroit Lions in the first round of the 1989 draft pick. Sanders donated a portion of the signing bonus of his multimillion dollar contract to his Baptist church back in Wichita.

As running back for the Lions, Sanders wrapped up his first year as a professional by being named NFL Rookie of the Year. He also had the honor of being chosen for the All-Pro team and starting running back for the National Football Conference in the Pro Bowl. Over the years, while the Lions had varying degrees of success—they fell one game short of the Super Bowl in 1991—Sanders was a consistently outstanding star and a decisive force in the team's offensive game. Furthermore, with his extraordinary quickness and massive, rock-solid legs, Sanders was considered one of the most difficult backs to tackle in the NFL.

Sanders was a committed athlete who trained rigorously throughout the year, subjecting himself to as much physical challenge off the field as on. A devoted Christian who conducted chapel services and Bible study groups for his teammates, Sanders was widely considered one of the greatest athletes ever to play football. In 1997 he became one of the highest paid players in the NFL when the Lions signed him to a five-year contract worth more than $34 million, but he took an early retirement in 1998. He was inducted into the Pro Football Hall of Fame in 2004.

GALE SAYERS

(b. 1943–)

Gale Eugene Sayers was born on May 30, 1943, in Wichita, Kansas. An African American collegiate and professional football player, Sayers was an explosive running back who played for the Chicago Bears (1965–71) of the National Football League (NFL). His exceptional career was shortened due to injuries.

He grew up in Omaha, Nebraska, where, as a high school player, he established himself as an outstanding break-away runner. He attended the University of Kansas and was twice named All-American (1963, 1964). In 1965 he was the Chicago Bears' top pick in the NFL draft.

In his first year as a professional, Sayers led the league in touchdowns (22) and scoring (132 points) and he also tied an NFL record, scoring 6 touchdowns in a single game. As a result he was the overwhelming favorite for the 1965 Rookie of the Year award. Regarded as one of the greatest open-field runners, he led the league in rushing in 1966 and 1969. He was named All-Pro from 1965 to 1969 and amassed a career total of 4,956 yards.

During the 1968 season Sayers suffered the first of several knee injuries. After several operations, he retired in 1971.

Following his retirement, Sayers served as athletic director at several universities, including Southern Illinois and Tennessee State. In 1977 he was inducted into the Professional Football Hall of Fame.

MARTIN SHERIDAN

(b. 1881–d. 1918)

Although he achieved his greatest success as a discus thrower, U.S. track and field athlete Martin Sheridan excelled in many events and is considered one of the best all-around athletes of the early 20th century. He won three Olympic gold medals and was a star at the 1906 Intercalated Games in Athens, Greece.

Martin Joseph Sheridan, often called Marty, was born on March 28, 1881, in Bohola, County Mayo, Ireland. He immigrated to the United States in 1897. Sheridan developed an interest in track and field through his brother, the Amateur Athletic Union (AAU) discus-throwing champion of 1901 and 1902. Sheridan himself won the AAU discus throw four times during his career. He also placed first in the all-around competition (the forerunner of the modern-day decathlon) in 1905, 1907, and 1909; in each contest, he set a new record for total points. In all, he earned 11 AAU titles.

Sheridan made his first Olympic appearance at the 1904 games in St. Louis, Missouri, and captured a gold medal in the discus throw. At the Intercalated Games, an unofficial Olympic contest held in 1906 in Athens, he repeated as the winner in the discus competition and earned a second gold medal in the shot put. He also won silver medals for the stone throw, standing high jump, and standing long jump and a bronze medal for the Greek-style discus throw. He was a favorite to earn a medal in the pentathlon as well, but he had to withdraw because of injury.

Sheridan successfully defended his discus-throwing title at the 1908 Olympics in London, England; he also placed first in the Greek-style discus throw and third in the standing long jump. In addition to his athletic accomplishments, Sheridan became known at the games for a comment he made to the press. Teammate Ralph Rose, who carried the flag in the opening ceremonies, took the advice of Sheridan and other athletes and did not dip the flag when passing the British royal box. Sheridan later told reporters, "This flag dips to no earthly king!"

During his athletic career Sheridan worked on the New York City police force and often acted as a personal bodyguard for the mayor. He died of pneumonia in 1918 in New York City on the eve of his 37th birthday. He was inducted into the National Track and Field Hall of Fame in 1988.

EMMITT SMITH

(b. 1969–)

In 2002 Emmitt Smith became the all-time leading rusher in National Football League (NFL) history. He retired after the 2004 season with 18,355 yards rushing. He also holds the record for most rushing touchdowns in a career, with 164.

Emmitt James Smith III was born on May 15, 1969 in Pensacola, Florida. He played football for three years (1987–89) at the University of Florida (in Gainesville), racking up 58 school records before being selected in the first round of the NFL draft by the Dallas Cowboys.

Smith soon proved himself as one of the league's best running backs. He was named NFL offensive Rookie of the Year in 1990 and the following season ran for 1,563 yards to capture the first of his four NFL rushing titles (the other three were in 1992, 1993, and 1995). He led the Cowboys to back-to-back Super Bowl wins following the 1992 and 1993 seasons. In 1993 he earned Most Valuable Player trophies for both the regular season and the Super Bowl. A third Super Bowl championship followed the 1995 season. After the 2002 season Smith was released by the Cowboys and signed by the Arizona Cardinals.

Though Smith was relatively small—he stood only 5 feet, 9 inches (1.75 meters) tall and weighed 212 pounds (96 kilograms)—and lacked great speed, he thrived in the NFL by relying on his strength, determination, and superb preparation. He ultimately proved to be one of the NFL's most sturdy players at any position (between 1990 and 2002 he failed to start in only two games). In 2010 he was inducted into the Pro Football Hall of Fame.

ANNIKA SÖRENSTAM

(b. 1970–)

The Swedish-born American golfer Annika Sörenstam was one of the most successful golfers in the history of the Ladies Professional Golf Association (LPGA).

Annika Sörenstam was born on October 9, 1970, in Stockholm, Sweden. She began playing golf at age 12, and she was a member of the Swedish national team from 1987 to 1992. She attended the University of Arizona, where she won a National Collegiate Athletic Association title in 1991 and earned All-America honors in 1991 and 1992. In 1992 she won the world amateur championship, finished second at the U.S. women's amateur championship, and posted the second lowest score among amateurs at the U.S. Women's Open. Sörenstam was the European tour's Rookie of the Year in 1993 and, with three top-10 finishes on the LPGA tour in 1994, was named that tour's Rookie of the Year as well. In 1995 she posted her first LPGA tour victory at the U.S. Women's Open and went on to win Player of the Year honors, a feat she would repeat seven additional times in the following 10 years. In 1998 Sörenstam became the first player on the LPGA tour to finish the season with a scoring average below 70 (69.99).

Sörenstam won eight LPGA events in 2001, including her second major tournament, the Kraft Nabisco Championship. That year she also became the first woman to shoot a 59 in a round of a professional tournament. She won 11 events in 2002, the most in the LPGA in nearly 40 years. In 2003 she won the LPGA Championship and the Women's British Open to complete the career Grand Slam. In 2003 Sörenstam also became the first woman to play in a men's Professional Golf Association tournament (the Bank of America Colonial Tournament in Fort Worth, Texas) since Babe Didrikson Zaharias in 1945.

Sörenstam broke her own single-season scoring average record in 2004 when she posted a mean score of 68.69 for the year while finishing in the top 10 in 16 of the 18 LPGA tournaments she entered. In 2006 Sörenstam won the U.S. Women's Open for her 10th career major title. Her play subsequently fell off, and she retired from competitive golf in 2008. Sörenstam was inducted into the World Golf Hall of Fame in 2003.

MARK SPITZ

(b. 1950–)

Mark Spitz won gold medals in all seven events in which he participated at the 1972 Olympics in Munich, Germany. He also managed to set world records in each event. Spitz's extraordinary performance at the 1972 games overshadowed his earlier showing at the 1968 Olympics in Mexico City, Mexico, where he won two gold medals, one silver, and a bronze medal.

Mark Andrew Spitz was born in Modesto, California, on February 10, 1950, and moved with his family to Honolulu, Hawaii, while he was still very young. Brought to the ocean as a toddler, Spitz showed an early enthusiasm for swimming while living in Hawaii. The family moved to Sacramento, California, where Spitz received his first formal swimming lessons at a local YMCA. By the time Spitz was 10 he had already set

17 records for his age group. With the coaching of George Haines of the Santa Clara Swim Club, Spitz was soon qualifying for national competitions.

He claimed four gold medals at his first international competition at the 1965 Maccabiah Games in Tel Aviv, Israel, which attracts Jewish contestants from many countries. In 1967 he set his first world record, swimming the 400-meter freestyle in 4 minutes, 10.6 seconds. Setting a total of six world records at international competitions during 1967, Spitz was honored by *Swimming World* magazine with a mention as World Swimmer of Year. At the 1968 Olympic trials Spitz qualified to compete in three individual events and three relays. Although many sports commentators considered Spitz the most promising member of the United States 1968 Olympic swim team, his performance failed to meet his supporters' high expectations. Of the six events in which Spitz competed, he won a silver medal for the 100-meter butterfly, a bronze for the 100-meter freestyle, and two gold medals as a member of relay teams.

Having graduated from Santa Clara High School earlier in 1968, Spitz returned from the Olympics to enroll in the pre-dental school at Indiana University in Bloomington, Indiana, which had a championship swim team coached by Jim Counsilman. While gaining strength in individual events, Spitz played a central role in continuing Indiana's winning streak at National Collegiate Athletic Association championships. In 1971 Spitz won two collegiate and four national championships, also setting two records in the United States and seven world records. He was recognized with a second Robert J.H. Kiphuth Award for individual achievement and received the 1971 Sullivan Award for his accomplishments as an amateur athlete.

By the beginning of 1972 Spitz held 35 United States records and 23 world records. Again a favorite for the 1972 Olympics, Spitz more than met expectations by winning an unmatched seven gold medals, surpassing a previous record of five gold medals won at a single Olympics by Italian fencer Nedo Nadi in 1920. On his first day of competition he won the 200-meter butterfly in 2 minutes, 0.7 seconds, setting a new world record. He also anchored the United States 400-meter relay team to a world record in 3 minutes, 26.42 seconds, bringing him a second gold

Mark Spitz, mid-stroke during the 200m butterfly event at the 1972 Olympics. Spitz won a gold medal in each event he entered during the Olympiad, held in Berlin. AFP/Getty Images

medal. In the next few days he added five more gold medals, swimming the 200-meter freestyle in 1 minute, 52.78 seconds; the 100-meter butterfly in 54.27 seconds; the 100-meter freestyle in 51.22 seconds; the 400-meter medley relay in 3 minutes, 48.16 seconds; and the 800-meter freestyle relay in 7 minutes, 35.78 seconds.

After the 1972 Olympics, Spitz finished his degree at Indiana University with the intention of entering dental school, but instead found work in the entertainment business as an actor and sports commentator, and then started a career in real estate. In 1973 he married Susan Wener, with whom he had a son. Although he retired from swimming competition in the 1970s, he took part in the United States Olympic swim trials in 1991 but did not make the team.

ROGER STAUBACH

(b. 1942–)

R oger Staubach was an American collegiate and professional football quarterback who was an important factor in the establishment of the National Football League (NFL) Dallas Cowboys as a dominant team in the 1970s.

Roger Thomas Staubach or "Roger the Dodger" was born on February 5, 1942, Cincinnati, Ohio. He played college football at the U.S. Naval Academy (1962–65), where as a quarterback he gained 4,253 yards (3,571 yards by passing) and scored 18 touchdowns. He was named All-American and won the Heisman Trophy as the best collegiate player in 1963. He served in the U.S. Navy (1965–69) following graduation from the academy.

During Staubach's career with the Cowboys (1969–79), they were in the play-offs every year but one (1974) and played in four Super Bowl games, winning in the 1971 and 1977 seasons. Staubach led the league in passer rating in four seasons (1971, 1973, 1978–79).

In his career, Staubach, known as "Captain Comeback," rallied the Cowboys to victory in 14 games in which, with two minutes to play, they were either tied or losing. His honest image and professional conduct, together with those of his coach, Tom Landry, were a major part of the Cowboys' characterization as "America's Team" in the 1970s. Staubach announced his retirement from football in 1979 and was briefly a sports announcer. He was inducted into the Pro Football Hall of Fame in 1985.

MICHAEL STRAHAN

(b. 1971–)

M ichael Anthony Strahan was born on November 21, 1971, in Houston, Texas. He is an American football player who, playing defensive end for the New York Giants proved himself as one of the best pass rushers in the history of the National Football League (NFL).

At age nine Strahan moved to Germany when his father, a major in the U.S. Army, was stationed there. As a result, the young Strahan played very little organized football growing up. A die-hard weight lifter, he became strong enough that his father believed he could earn a college football scholarship, so Strahan was sent to live with his uncle (a former NFL player) in Houston before his senior year of high school. He played well enough to win a scholarship to Texas Southern University, which competed in lower-division college football. Strahan set a school record with 41.5 sacks in his four years at Texas Southern and was selected by the Giants in the 1993 NFL draft.

After the 2000 regular season, Strahan helped the Giants reach Super Bowl XXXV, which the team lost to the Baltimore Ravens. In 2001 he recorded 22.5 sacks, an NFL single-season record, and was named the NFL's Defensive Player of the Year. He again led the league in sacks in 2003, totaling 18.5 over the course of the season. Strahan and the Giants advanced to another Super Bowl in February 2008, where they upset the previously undefeated New England Patriots. He retired months after that surprise victory, ending his career with seven Pro Bowl selections and four first-team All-Pro honors.

The fun-loving Strahan had long been a popular commercial spokesman, and his famous gap-toothed smile became well known to American television audiences. His profitable endorsement sideline career continued after his retirement, and he also acted on a number of television shows. In 2012 he became the cohost of the syndicated talk show *Live! With Kelly and Michael.*

SHERYL SWOOPES

(b. 1971–)

Sheryl Swoopes is an American basketball player who won three Women's National Basketball Association (WNBA) Most Valuable Player (MVP) awards (2000, 2002, 2005) and four WNBA titles (1997–2000) as a member of the Houston Comets.

Sheryl Denise Swoopes was born March 25, 1971, in Brownfield, Texas. After being named the 1991 national Junior College Player of the Year, Swoopes transferred to Texas Tech University. There she won the National Player of the Year award in her senior season as she led the Lady Raiders to the 1993 National Collegiate Athletic Association national championship (where Swoopes set a record for most points scored in the title game, with 47).

She joined the Comets before the WNBA's inaugural campaign in 1997, and she helped the team win that season's WNBA title. Swoopes and the Comets won three additional championships in the next three years, the last of which (in 2000) came after a regular season in which she scored a career-high 20.7 points per game and won the league's MVP and Defensive Player of the Year awards. Swoopes won both the MVP and Defensive Player of the Year awards again in 2002. She repeated as Defensive Player of the Year in 2003 after leading the league in steals per game, and in 2005 she became the league's first three-time MVP.

In 2005 Swoopes made national news when she revealed that she was gay, becoming the most prominent athlete in a North American team sport to do so. (However, in 2011, she announced her engagement to a man.) A back injury limited her to appearances in just three games in 2007, and in 2008 she joined the Seattle Storm but was released at the end of the season. Swoopes played with the Greek team Esperides in 2010 and joined the WNBA's Tulsa Shock in 2011. She did not return to professional basketball in 2012.

Swoopes was a five-time All-WNBA first-team selection, and she won three Olympic gold medals as a member of the U.S. women's basketball team (1996, 2000, and 2004).

LAWRENCE TAYLOR

(b. 1959–)

Lawrence Taylor is an American collegiate and professional football player, considered one of the best linebackers in the history of the game. As a member of the New York Giants of the National Football League (NFL), he won Super Bowl championships following the 1986 and 1990 seasons.

Lawrence Julius Taylor, or "L.T.," was born on February 4, 1959, in Williamsburg, Virginia. Taylor, who did not play organized football until the 11th grade, attended the University of North Carolina, where he initially played defensive lineman before being moved to outside linebacker. With a rare combination of size and speed, Taylor, 6 feet, 3 inches (1.91 meters) tall and weighing 240 pounds (109 kg), excelled as a linebacker, and he was named All-American in 1980.

Taylor entered the NFL draft in 1981 and was the second overall pick, selected by the New York Giants. By the end of his first professional season, he had 9.5 quarterback sacks (an unofficial number, since the NFL did not keep statistics on sacks until the following season) and a reputation for making hard, vicious hits. He was named Rookie of the Year and Defensive Player of the Year, an honor that he received again the following season. In 1986 he led the league with 20.5 sacks, guided the Giants to victory over the Denver Broncos in Super Bowl XXI, and was named Most Valuable Player of the NFL—the second defensive player in league history to receive the honor. Taylor and the Giants won a second championship in January 1991, defeating the Buffalo Bills in Super Bowl XXV.

Taylor revolutionized the play of outside linebacker, traditionally a "read and react" position (the linebacker would watch the play develop, then move to stop it). Taylor was an attacking linebacker who possessed the strength and speed to make plays anywhere on the field. He was the most disruptive defensive player of his era. During his 13-year career, he was named All-Pro six times (1981–87) and made 10 Pro Bowl appearances (1981–90 seasons). He retired from professional football after the 1993 season with career totals of 132.5 sacks (not including sacks from his rookie year), 1,088 tackles, 33 forced fumbles, and 9 interceptions. He was voted into the Pro Football Hall of Fame in 1999.

Taylor's life off the field was troubled both during and after his football career. He struggled with a cocaine addiction, and in 1988 he was suspended by the NFL for failing a drug test. Between 1996 and 1998 he was arrested three times on drug charges. After completing a rehabilitation program in 1998, he pursued a career in acting. Taylor's *LT: Over the Edge* (2003; cowritten with Steve Serby) detailed his roller-coaster past. In May 2010 he was arrested and charged with third-degree rape and solicitation of a prostitute after he allegedly had sexual relations with a 16-year-old girl at a hotel in Suffern, New York. In January 2011 he pleaded guilty to sexual misconduct and patronizing a prostitute, both misdemeanor charges, and was sentenced to six years of probation.

JIM THORPE

(b. 1888–d. 1953)

Jim Thorpe was one of the greatest athletes in American history, especially in football and baseball. He was mainly of American Indian descent. The issue of whether he was wrong or wronged arose after Thorpe achieved the amazing feat of winning gold medals in both the pentathlon and the decathlon in the 1912 Olympic Games in Stockholm, Sweden. It was discovered that he had played semiprofessional baseball in the summers of 1909 and 1910. He was stripped of his amateur status by the Amateur Athletic Union, and he was deprived of his honors.

Jim Thorpe was born near Prague, Indian Territory (now Oklahoma), on May 28, 1888. His athletic ability gained him entrance to the Carlisle Indian School in Pennsylvania in 1907. There, under Coach Pop Warner, he helped make the school a football powerhouse. This, followed by his Olympic successes, gained him international recognition.

Thorpe left Carlisle in 1913 and played professional baseball for the next several years. He was with the New York Giants from 1913 to 1915, the Cincinnati Reds to 1917, and the Giants again to 1919. Thorpe finished his baseball career with the Boston Braves in 1919. He also played professional football, mostly with the Canton Bulldogs.

By 1920, when the National Football League was formed, Thorpe's career was approaching an end, though he made an appearance as late as 1929 with the Chicago (now Phoenix) Cardinals. He was, however, the most famous football player in the nation. For a year he served as the first president of the new league.

In later years he fell on hard times and was often unable to find work. After his retirement from sports in 1929, he appeared in carnivals, worked as a stuntman in motion pictures, and occasionally lectured. In 1950 he was named the greatest football player and greatest male athlete of the first half of the century by Associated Press polls. A film biography was released in 1951.

Thorpe was elected to many halls of fame, including those of college and professional football and track and field. After his death his children fought for the restoration of his Olympic awards. In 1973 the Amateur Athletic Union restored his amateur standing for the years 1909 to 1912. In 1982 the International Olympic Committee returned the awards.

Thorpe died in Lomita, California, on March 28, 1953, and he was buried in a Pennsylvania town renamed in his honor.

YANI TSENG

(b. 1989–)

In 2011, Yani Tseng cemented her status as the dominant player on the Ladies Professional Golf Association (LPGA) tour. In June she displayed a superb performance at the LPGA Championship, winning the tournament by 10 strokes. Her 19-under-par 269 tied the record-low score at an LPGA major. In July she won the Women's British Open for the second consecutive year, edging American Brittany Lang by four strokes. The victory gave Tseng—at just 22 years of age—her fifth career major tournament title and made her the youngest golfer of either sex to reach that milestone.

Yani Tseng was born on January 23, 1989, in Guishan, Taiwan. She played golf from the age of six and by her early teens was an accomplished amateur. In 2002 she won the girls 13–14 age division at the Callaway junior world golf championships, and two years later she captured the U.S. Women's Amateur Public Links title. She turned professional in 2007 and joined the LPGA tour the following year. At the 2008 LPGA Championship, she beat Maria Hjorth of Sweden in a four-hole play-off to become Taiwan's first major golf champion. Tseng also recorded five second-place finishes during her inaugural season on the tour and received the LPGA's Rookie of the Year award.

In 2010 Tseng added two major titles to her collection. At the Kraft Nabisco Championship in early April, she shot a 13-under-par 275 to secure a one-stroke victory over Suzann Pettersen of Norway. Later in the year Tseng also triumphed at the Women's British Open, again finishing on top by a single stroke, this time over Katherine Hull of Australia. At the conclusion of the season, Tseng was recognized as the LPGA's Player of the Year, becoming the second youngest player (behind American Nancy Lopez) to be given the honor.

In February 2011, after winning several tournaments at the beginning of the season, Tseng rose to the top of the women's world rankings. By April she had become the youngest women's golfer to surpass the $5 million mark in career earnings. Tseng achieved six wins on the LPGA tour during the season, notching her final victory in October at the Hana Bank Championship in Inch'on, South Korea. That month she was named again as the LPGA Player of the Year. Tseng was only the eighth player in history to have won the award in consecutive seasons.

ABBY WAMBACH

(b. 1980–)

Abby Wambach is considered to be one of the most dominant and effective players in the field of soccer. Born and brought up in Rochester, New York, Wombach took her first steps in the field of soccer at the ripe age of four, where she played in her first youth league. Upon scoring an incredible 27 goals across a span of merely three games, she was transferred to a boys' team to further enhance her exemplary skills.

Wambach continued playing soccer in high school and also took up basketball, after which her sole focus was on soccer at the University of Florida. There, she gathered many accolades, such as being named All-SEC for four seasons in a row, two-time winner of the Conference Player of the Year, and First-Team NSCAA All-American. During her senior season, she also helped the Gators reach the NCAA Final Four. She broke all records in school by scoring 96 goals, 24 game-winning goals, 10 hat tricks, 49 assists, and an incredible 241 points.

Her incredible performance was noticed by U-21 National Team coach Jerry Smith in 2001. He helped her secure a position on the senior national spot. In 2002, she was the second player to be taken in the WUSA draft, where she was teammates with Mia Hamm on the Washington

Freedom. By 2003, the duo was WUSA's most dangerous scoring pair, winning a combined 66 points that helped the Freedom clinch the league title.

Wambach also began nine of 14 WNT games that year, which included five Women's World Cup matches where she helped the U.S. secure a third-place win and earned the title of U.S. Soccer's Female Athlete of the Year.

Two thousand four was one of Wambach's best seasons in the history of the U.S. Women's National Team. Her header in extra time of the U.S. and Brazil's 2004 Olympic Games gold medal match in Athens enabled her team to defeat Brazil with a

Abby Wambach (No. 16), celebrating with teammate Julie Foudy after scoring the winning goal against Brazil in the women's soccer gold medal match of the 2004 Summer Olympic Games. Shaun Botterill/Getty Images

2–1 score and win the gold. In the same year, she became the fourth U.S. player to score double-figured goals and assists in the same year, with a score of 31 goals across 30 matches. She collected 75 points over the year, the second highest total, succeeded only in 1991 by Michelle Akers. This also earned her the title of U.S. Soccer Female Athlete of the Year for the second time in a row.

In 2007, Wambach made her way to fifth place in the all-time U.S. goal-scoring list. She helped the U.S. head to the World Cup with 11 goals and 3 assists. While playing in the World Cup, she collided with a North Korean player during the first game and suffered an injury, resulting in 11 stitches to her head. Despite that, she managed to score 6 goals in 6 matches, helping her country win third place and reaching her 100-cap milestone during the quarterfinal match against England.

During the course of the next year, she scored 13 goals, 10 assists, and 36 points. However, during her team's pre-Olympics final match, she collided with a Brazilian opponent and damaged her tibia and fibula. This put an end to her Olympic performance and left her a goal short of reaching 100 career goals.

Wambach took a break to recover from her injuries but was soon back with both the Washington Freedom and the U.S. National Team. Her goal against Canada in her hometown match helped her cross the 100-goal mark, making her the ninth female player in the world to achieve this record. She now ranks fifth among U.S. players while holding the best goal per game ratio in the history of U.S. soccer.

JERRY WEST

(b. 1938–)

Jerry West is an American basketball player, coach, and general manager. He spent four noteworthy decades with the Los Angeles Lakers of the National Basketball Association (NBA).

Jerome Alan West was born on May 28, 1938, in Cheylan, West Virginia. Weak as a child, West overcame his early physical limitations by putting in long hours practicing his shot and developing the quick release that would become his signature. He grew considerably during the summer before his senior year and then led his high school to a state championship, drawing the attention of colleges nationwide.

As a sharpshooting 6-foot 3-inch (1.91-metre) guard for West Virginia University, West became the school's all-time leading scorer and rebounder, and he was twice named an All-American (1959, 1960).

West was drafted by the Lakers with the second overall pick of the 1960 NBA draft. The quiet West was initially thought by some to be an ill fit for Los Angeles, but he readily adapted to the L.A. media spotlight and proved to be one of the most popular figures in franchise history. (His early sarcastic nickname "Zeke from Cabin Creek" was not even an accurate reference to his proper hometown of Cheylan but rather referred to a nearby unincluded area.) West soon came to be known as "Mr. Clutch." He had a career scoring average of 27.0 points per game, failing to average more than 20 points per game in just his rookie season, and he was named an All-Star in each of his 14 seasons in the league. As amazing as his individual achievements were, his Lakers teams did not reach a similar level of success in an era dominated by the Boston Celtics.

West led his team to nine berths in the NBA finals, but the Lakers won just one championship (1972). In addition to his professional and collegiate achievements, West was a member of the U.S. men's basketball team that won the gold medal at the Rome 1960 Olympic Games.

After his retirement in 1974, he served as the Lakers' head coach for three seasons (1976–79), guiding them to 145 wins and 101 losses over that span. West then spent three years as a scout for the Lakers before becoming the team's general manager in 1982. He shaped squads that won five NBA titles between 1982 and 2000, his final year with the franchise. West worked in the front office of the Memphis Grizzlies from 2002 to 2007, assembling the first play-off teams for the young franchise. His front-office insights led to two NBA Executive of the Year awards (1995, 2004). In 2011 he became an adviser to the Golden State Warriors, as well as a member of the team's executive board. West was inducted into the Naismith Memorial Basketball Hall of Fame in 1980, and in 1996 he was named one of the 50 greatest players in NBA history. The greatest testament to his long-term impact on the sport of basketball is perhaps the fact that a photo of West served as the model for the famous red, white, and blue NBA logo.

SERENA WILLIAMS

(b. 1981–)

American tennis player Serena Williams was a major force in her sport in the early twenty-first century. Possessing a strong forehand, a fast, aggressive serve, and superb athleticism, she changed the women's professional game with her powerful playing style.

Williams was born on September 26, 1981, in Saginaw, Michigan. She and her older sister Venus were introduced to tennis at age four by their father, Richard, whose stated goal was to raise them to be champions. The sisters' unlikely ascent began on rough public courts in

Los Angeles, California. Both girls played exhibition matches against leading professionals before they reached their teens. In 1991 the family moved to Florida, where the sisters enrolled in a tennis academy.

Williams's professional debut came in 1995. Two years later, in only her fifth professional tournament, she beat Mary Pierce, ranked seventh, and Monica Seles, ranked fourth, to reach the semifinals at the Ameritech Cup in Chicago. At number 304, Williams was the lowest-ranked player ever to have beaten two top-ten players in the same tournament. After the competition, her world singles ranking soared to 102.

Expectations for Williams began to grow quickly. Her father made bold statements to the media about his talented daughters, who both signed multimillion-dollar endorsement deals. Less than a year later, in June 1998, Williams reached the top 20. In April 1999, after defeating Amelie Mauresmo to win the Paris Indoor Open, Steffi Graf to win the Indian Wells masters tournament, and Martina Hingis in the semifinals at the Lipton Championship, Williams broke the top ten at number nine.

The 17-year-old champion reached the top five at number four after winning the U.S. Open later that year. As the tournament's seventh seed, Williams was the lowest-seeded woman to win the U.S. Open title since the beginning of the open era in 1968 and the second African American woman to win a Grand Slam event, after Althea Gibson's victories in 1957–58.

Williams captured three more Grand Slam titles in 2002, winning the French Open, Wimbledon, and the U.S. Open and defeating Venus in the finals of each tournament. Although Serena had finished the 2000 and 2001 seasons ranked sixth, after her French Open victory in 2002 she climbed to number two, behind only Venus. The Williams sisters were the first siblings ever to occupy the top two spots in the world rankings at the same time. On July 8, 2002, after winning the Wimbledon title, Serena overtook Venus in the rankings for the top spot. In 2003 Serena won the Australian Open and Wimbledon, again besting her sister in the finals. She won the Australian Open four more times (2005, 2007, 2009, and 2010) and captured the U.S. Open title for the third time in 2008.

In 2009 Serena earned her third Wimbledon singles title, once again defeating her sister, and successfully defended the title in 2010. Serena subsequently battled various health issues that kept her off the court for almost a year. In 2012 she won her fifth Wimbledon singles title and fourth U.S. Open title. In 2013 Serena won her second French Open singles championship.

The Williams sisters broke records also as a formidable doubles team. At the 2000 Olympic Games in Sydney, Australia, their convincing 6–1, 6–1 victory over the Dutch team made them the first sisters ever to win a gold medal in doubles competition. The sisters won gold again in the doubles event at the 2008 Games in Beijing, China, and at the 2012 Games in London, England, where Serena also claimed the singles gold medal. In addition, the sisters captured doubles titles at all four Grand Slam tournaments—the U.S. Open in 1999 and 2009, the French Open in 1999 and 2010, Wimbledon in 2000, 2002, 2008, 2009, and 2012, and the Australian Open in 2001, 2003, 2009, and 2010.

U.S. tennis star Serena Williams, volleying during a 2011 match in Eastbourne, England. Mike Hewitt/Getty Images

TED WILLIAMS

(b. 1918–d. 2002)

Had it not been for five years of military service during his prime playing years, Ted Williams might well have broken Babe Ruth's career home run record of 714. As it was, Williams achieved a total of 521 home runs during his playing career with the Boston Red Sox from 1939 until 1960. He played in 2,292 games, was at bat 7,706 times, got 2,654 hits, and ended his career with a lifetime average of .344. Williams's season average of .406 in 1941 was the highest since Rogers Hornsby's .424 in 1924, and it has not been exceeded by any player in either major league.

Theodore Samuel Williams was born on August 30, 1918, in San Diego, California. After playing baseball in high school, Williams began his professional career in 1935 with the San Diego Padres of the old Pacific Coast League. In 1937 he was sold to the Boston Red Sox, and after two years on their farm team, the Minneapolis Millers, he was brought up to play in Boston. He was named Rookie of the Year in his first season.

When the United States entered World War II, Williams joined the Marines, where he served as an aviator. He also saw service in the Korean War. In his 19 years with the Red Sox he led the American League in batting six times, the last time in 1958 when he was 40 years old. He led the league four times in home runs and in runs batted in. In the 1946 All-Star game he got five hits, two of them home runs. He retired from playing on September 28, 1960. He was elected to the Baseball Hall of Fame in 1966.

Williams returned to baseball in 1969 as manager and part owner of the Washington Senators. When the team moved to Texas in 1972 as the Texas Rangers, he left managing. He had become convinced that players did not take hitting as seriously as they should. His autobiography, *My Turn at Bat*, was published in 1969, and his *The Science of Hitting* came out in 1971. He died on July 5, 2002, in Inverness, Florida.

VENUS WILLIAMS

(b. 1980–)

An aggressive will to win and a strong all-around game described Venus Williams well. At the age of 17 the unseeded, relatively unknown player became the first African American to reach the women's singles finals of the U.S. Open since Althea Gibson claimed the title in 1958. When Williams won the singles title at Wimbledon in 2000, she was likewise the first African American woman to do so since Gibson won in 1958. Williams became the top-ranked woman tennis player in the world in 2002.

Venus Ebony Starr Williams was born on June 17, 1980, in Lynwood, California. Introduced to tennis when she was just a toddler, Williams pursued her interest in the game on public courts in her hometown of Compton, California, a Los Angeles suburb troubled by gangs and violent crime. She and her sister Serena were coached almost exclusively by their parents, neither of whom had any formal tennis training. In 1991 the family moved to Fort Lauderdale, Florida, where Rick Macci, the professional coach who developed Jennifer Capriati's game, coached the sisters.

Steered by her father, Williams left junior competition at age 11 to concentrate on school. Whereas most young players are well seasoned in junior competition by the time they enter professional tournaments, Williams entered the professional tour in 1994 at age 14 with relatively little experience in match play. Her parents invested in her a strong sense of self-confidence, which grew into an undaunted will to win. An exceptionally tall player, Williams had to bend her knees deeply to return an opponent's slices. Her powerful serve was clocked at more than 100 miles (160 kilometers) per hour.

Williams entered the 1997 U.S. Open ranked number 66 by the Women's Tennis Association (WTA). She was the first unseeded woman ever to reach a U.S. Open singles finals since the open era began in 1968 and the first woman to reach a U.S. Open final in her debut since Pam Shriver advanced to the final in 1978 at age 16. Williams lost in the finals to 16-year-old, first-seeded Martina Hingis, but Williams's WTA ranking improved to number 27.

139

In March 1998 Williams claimed her first professional singles title at the IGA Tennis Classic. Later that month she defeated top-ranked Hingis in the semifinals and then Anna Kournikova in the finals to capture the $1.9 million Lipton Championship. By this, Williams became the first U.S.-born woman to win the tournament since Chris Evert did so in 1986. After Williams's victory, her ranking rose to number ten.

After Serena entered the professional tour, the sisters' singles careers often set them against one another. Although Serena was the first of the pair to win a Grand Slam singles title, at the 1999 U.S. Open, Venus followed with a victory at Wimbledon in 2000. She defeated Serena in the semifinals and Lindsay Davenport in the finals, both in straight sets. At that year's U.S. Open, Venus triumphed over first-ranked Hingis and then second-ranked Davenport to take the title. She won her second Wimbledon and U.S. Open championships in 2001. She ended both the 2000 and 2001 seasons ranked third in the world. In February 2002 she became the tenth woman ever to hold the number one spot. Later that year Serena defeated her in the finals round of the French Open, Wimbledon, and the U.S. Open, and Serena overtook her in the world rankings. Venus won Wimbledon again in 2005, 2007, and 2008.

The Williams sisters also played doubles tournaments together, capturing titles at all four Grand Slam events: the U.S. Open (1999 and 2009), the French Open (1999 and 2010), Wimbledon (2000, 2002, 2008, 2009, and 2012), and the Australian Open (2001, 2003, 2009, and 2010). At the 2000 Olympic Games in Sydney, Australia, the sisters won a gold medal in the doubles competition, and Venus took the gold in singles. The sisters also won the doubles gold medal at the 2008 Olympics in Beijing, China, and at the 2012 Olympics in London, England.

TIGER WOODS

(b. 1975–)

Tiger Woods stunned the golfing world by winning three consecutive United States Amateur golf titles and two professional tournaments by the age of 20. By the age of 28 he had achieved worldwide fame by winning eight major championship titles and a total of 39 Professional Golfers' Association (PGA) tournaments—an accomplishment unmatched in the history of golf. Because of his youth, talent, and ethnically mixed heritage, Woods also was recognized for setting new standards of competition and variety in the sport.

Eldrick Woods was born on December 30, 1975, in Cypress, California, near Los Angeles. He was given the nickname "Tiger" by his father, Earl, in honor of a friend who had saved Earl's life during the Vietnam War. When Tiger was only 18 months old, his father gave him a sawed-off golf club. By the time he was a toddler he had already gained fame for his skills by putting against entertainer Bob Hope on a national television show. By the age of 11 he was undefeated in more than 30 Southern California junior tournaments.

With his parents carefully guiding his career, between 1991 and 1993 Tiger won three consecutive United States Junior Amateur titles, something no one else had ever done. At 16, he was the youngest person to play in a PGA tournament. He then moved on to become the youngest person to win the United States Amateur and the first person to win both the Junior and the Amateur titles. He was only 20 in 1996 when he won his third consecutive Amateur title.

Tiger Woods's ethnic heritage made him even more exceptional in a sport traditionally ruled by white men. His dark skin caused him to be excluded from some private golf clubs while growing up, and many named him the first African American to achieve his golfing milestones. He is actually of African American, Native American, Asian, and Caucasian background.

Despite his busy golfing schedule, Tiger was an honor student in high school and attended Stanford University in California for two years before leaving college to join the professional golfing tour. Two weeks after he turned professional, the Nike company agreed to pay Woods more than $40 million in exchange for a five-year endorsement contract.

As a rookie on the tour, Woods was victorious in two out of his first seven professional tournaments, something no rookie had ever come close to achieving. In April 1997 Woods won his first major tournament—the Masters in Augusta, Georgia. At 21, he was the youngest player to win the green jacket, the award for victory at the championship. His four-round total of an 18-under-par 270 broke the tournament record of 271, set by Jack Nicklaus in 1965. Woods's winning margin of 12 shots shattered the old record of nine, also set by Nicklaus in 1965. He was the first golfer of color to win a major tournament.

The 2000 professional golf season added to Woods's growing reputation as the most dominant player in golf history. Woods won the United States Open at the famed Pebble Beach golf course by a record 15 strokes over his nearest challenger. In his next record-breaking performance he won the British Open at the ancestral home of golf in St. Andrews, Scotland. His total four-round score of 269 (19 strokes under par) was both a British Open and a major championship record. Woods then captured his third major victory of the year by winning the PGA Championship in a three-hole play-off. By the end of the year he had won a total of nine PGA tournaments and had earned more than $8.2 million in prize money, the most money ever won in a single season.

At the age of 24, Woods became the youngest golfer in history to achieve a career Grand Slam by winning all four of the professional tour's major championships. His career Grand Slam victories included the 1997 Masters, the 1999 PGA Championship, the 2000 United States Open, and the 2000 British Open. He joined the legendary group of Ben Hogan, Jack Nicklaus, Gary Player, and Gene Sarazen as the only professional golfers to win career Grand Slams.

In the spring of 2001 Woods continued his major tournament streak by winning his second Masters. With the Masters victory he became the first professional golfer in history to win all four major championship titles within a one-year period (running from June 2000 to May 2001). Woods won two more major titles in 2002—his third Masters and his second United States Open. After only eight years as a professional golfer, Woods had won eight major tournaments, had received the PGA's Player of the Year award six times, and had garnered more than $40 million in career earnings.

In 2005, after a drought of 10 winless major tournaments, Woods won the Masters and the British Open. He dominated the tour the following year, winning nine events, including the British Open and the PGA Championship. In 2007 he defended his title at the latter tournament to claim his 13th major championship. Some two months after undergoing knee surgery in 2008, Woods captured his third U.S. Open title in his first tournament back on the tour, completing his third career Grand Slam, a feat matched only by Nicklaus. Woods's dramatic U.S. Open victory—which involved an 18-hole play-off round followed by a sudden-death play-off—aggravated the damage to his knee, and the following week he withdrew from the remainder of the 2008 golf season in order to have more-extensive knee surgery. His return to the sport in 2009 featured a number of tournament wins but no major titles for the first time since 2004. Also in 2009, Woods's unprecedented streak of having never lost a major tournament when leading or co-leading after 54 holes was broken at 14 when he lost the PGA Championship after being ahead by two strokes before the final round.

In November 2009 Woods was involved in an early morning one-car accident outside his home in Orlando, Florida. The unusual circumstances of the crash led to a great deal of media scrutiny into his personal life. It was revealed that Woods, who had married Elin Nordegren in 2004, had a number of extramarital affairs, and his infidelity—which clashed with his solid-citizen reputation that had helped him earn hundreds of millions of dollars in endorsements over the years—became national news. The following month, Woods announced that he was taking an indefinite leave from golf in order to spend more time with his family.

He returned to the sport in April 2010 at the Masters Tournament. While Woods finished in the top five at both the Masters and the U.S. Open, his 2010 golf season was a disappointment that included no tournament wins and the worst four-round score of his professional career. In addition, he and Nordegren divorced in August of that year.

Woods's difficulties on the golf course continued in 2011 as he failed to win an official PGA tournament. His drought finally ended on March 25, 2012, when he won the Arnold Palmer Invitational, his first PGA victory in almost 30 months.

CY YOUNG

(b. 1867–d. 1955)

When he retired in 1911 after a record 22 seasons, baseball player Cy Young had won 511 major league games, more than any other pitcher. He played for the Cleveland Spiders from 1890 to 1898, the St. Louis Cardinals from 1899 to 1900, the Boston Red Sox from 1901 to 1908, the Cleveland Indians from 1909 to 1911, and the Boston Braves in 1911.

Denton True Young was born on March 29, 1867, in Gilmore, Ohio. He pitched 750 complete games and 7,356 innings, including a stretch of 23 consecutive hitless innings in 1904. He recorded 76 shutouts and three no-hit, no-run games, including modern baseball's first perfect game, on May 5, 1904. Elected to the Baseball Hall of Fame in 1937, he is also remembered in the Cy Young Award for best major league pitcher each year.

BABE DIDRIKSON ZAHARIAS

(b. 1911–d. 1956)

Babe Didrikson Zaharias was the outstanding American woman athlete of the 20th century. She performed in basketball, track and field, and golf. She turned to golf as a form of relaxation in 1932, but in a few years she became the United States' leading woman golfer.

Mildred Ella Didriksen (she later changed the spelling) was born in Port Arthur, Texas, on June 26, 1911. She became an All-American basketball player in 1930 and 1931. In 1932, at the women's annual track and field tournament sponsored by the Amateur Athletic Union, she entered eight events and won five.

In the 1932 Summer Olympics in Los Angeles she won gold medals for the javelin throw and the 80-meter hurdles, in both of which she set records. She was deprived of a gold medal in the high jump because of a technicality. She also excelled in softball, baseball, swimming, figure

Multi-sport athlete Babe Didrikson Zaharias, preparing to throw the javelin at the 1932 Olympic Games in Los Angeles, California. Hulton Archive/Getty Images

skating, billiards, and even football. After the 1932 Olympic Games she turned professional and took part in exhibitions throughout the country.

Didrikson began to play golf casually in 1932, but after 1934 she played the game exclusively. She soon became the leading amateur woman golfer in the United States. In 1946 she won the United States Women's Amateur tournament.

In 1947 Didrikson won 17 straight golf championships and became the first American winner of the British Ladies' Amateur. She became a professional golfer in 1948, and in 1950 she won the United States Women's Open. From 1948 through 1951 Didrikson was the leading money winner among women golfers. In 1954 she won the Open again as well as the All-American Open.

Didrikson married professional wrestler George Zaharias in 1938. In 1953 she underwent cancer surgery, which proved to have been unsuccessful and had to be repeated in 1956. She died that year on September 27, in Galveston, Tex. Her autobiography, *This Life I've Led*, in which she falsely claimed she was born in 1914, was published in 1955. A television movie of her life entitled *Babe* was made in 1975.

EMIL ZATOPEK

(b. 1922–d. 2000)

A distance runner, Emil Zatopek recorded one of the most memorable performances in Olympic history in 1952. Referred to as one of the greatest distance runners in the history of track and field competition, he won four Olympic gold medals.

Emil Zatopek was born on September 19, 1922, in Koprivnice, Northern Moravia, in Czechoslovakia (now in the Czech Republic). As a young man, Zatopek was forced to put aside his dreams of an athletic career to serve in the Czechoslovakian army during World War II. He eventually became an officer. Following the war, he resumed his distance training in time to compete in the 1948 Olympic Games in London and was favored to win the 5,000-meter run.

Zatopek, in something of an upset, finished second in the 5,000 but scored a surprise victory in the 10,000 meters to collect his first gold medal. Zatopek ran as if he were in agony, his face twisted in pain as if each step would be his last. Spectators marveled at the constant grimace on his face nearly as much as they did at his athletic ability.

In races ranging from 5,000 to 30,000 meters, Zatopek set 18 world records over the course of his career. Going into the 1952 Olympic Games in Helsinki, Finland, he was widely accepted as the supreme distance runner in the world. This view proved to be accurate as Zatopek delivered one of the most memorable Olympic performances of all time. Zatopek was under pressure to defend his title in the 10,000 meters and was also the favorite to win the 5,000. Zatopek won the gold in the 5,000 and, a few days later, the 10,000-meter event. He completed his amazing performance by winning the marathon, a race he had never run in competition, only three days after the 10,000, thereby pulling off the nearly impossible feat of recording a "triple." Not only was Zatopek the first runner to win the distance events, he set Olympic records in each race and set a new world mark in the marathon.

Those who witnessed Zatopek's amazing victories claimed it was the most inspired athletic exhibition that they had ever witnessed. Zatopek shrugged off the acclaim and later referred to the marathon as a "boring race."

Zatopek was much sought after as a coach around the world. At home, he supported the 1968 Prague Spring reform efforts in Czechoslovakia and fought for greater freedom and better living standards for the people. When the movement was put down, he was stripped of his army rank and of his membership in the Communist Party and for several years was forbidden to leave the country. From 1970 he worked with the Czechoslovak Physical Training Association and by the late 1970s was associated with the Czech national sports institute. With the end of the Cold War he received a public apology from the government. Zatopek died on November 22, 2000, in Prague.

GLOSSARY

ARBITRATION Settling of differences between parties by a person or persons chosen or agreed to by them.

DISPUTE To engage in an argument or debate.

DOMINATED To rule over; govern; control.

DRAMATIC Highly effective; striking.

ELITE Persons of the highest class.

EXUBERANT Describes an extremely joyful and vigorous, energetic, alert person.

POWERHOUSE A person or group having great energy, strength, or potential for success.

PROLIFIC Very productive and fruitful.

PROVINCIAL Belonging to a particular place; local.

REHABILITATE To restore to a condition of good health.

ROOKIE An athlete playing his or her first season as a member of a professional sports team.

SPANNED Reached a distance or amount.

FOR MORE INFORMATION

Canadian Football League
50 Wellington Street East, 3rd Floor
Toronto, ON Canada M5E 1C8
(416) 322-9650
Web site: http://www.cfl.ca
The CFL is the highest level of football competition in Canada. It
consists of eight teams divided into two groups of four called the
East Division and the West Division.

Canadian Hockey Association
151 Canada Olympic Road SW, Suite 201
Calgary, AB Canada T3B 6B7
(403) 777-3636
Web site: http://www.hockeycanada.ca
Hockey Canada oversees all operations of ice hockey in Canada,
including amateur, university, and professional competitions. It is
also a member of the International Ice Hockey Federation.

Fédération Internationale de Natation (FINA)
Avenue de l'Avant-Poste 4
1005 Lausanne, Switzerland
Web site: http://www.fina.org
FINA, the International Swimming Federation, administers international competitions in aquatics. FINA currently oversees competition in five aquatics sports, namely swimming, diving, synchro-
nized swimming, water polo, and open water swimming.

Major League Baseball
245 Park Avenue
New York, NY 10167
(212) 931-7800
Web site: http://www.mlb.com
Major League Baseball (MLB) is a professional baseball league,
earlier made up of teams that play in the American League and
National League. The two leagues merged in 2000 into a single

organization led by the Commissioner of Baseball. The league consists of 30 teams

National Basketball Association
NBA Corporate Office & Headquarters
645 Fifth Avenue
New York NY 10022
(212) 407-8000
Web site: http://www.nba.com
The National Basketball Association (NBA) is the preeminent men's professional basketball league in North America and is widely considered to be the premier men's professional basketball league in the world. It has 30 franchised member clubs (29 in the United States and 1 in Canada).

National Football League
345 Park Avenue
New York, NY 10154
Web site: http://www.nfl.com
The National Football League (NFL) is a professional American football league composed of 32 teams divided equally between the National Football Conference (NFC) and the American Football Conference (AFC). The champions of the NFC and AFC play the Super Bowl, one of the most watched sporting events in the world.

WEB SITES

Due to the changing nature of Internet links, Rosen Publishing has developed an online list of Web sites related to the subject of this book. This site is updated regularly. Please use this link to access the list:

http://www.rosenlinks.com/pysk/athlet

FOR FURTHER READING

Agassi, Andre. *Open: An Autobiography*. New York, NY: AKA Publishing, 2009.

Bolt, Usain. *Fastest Man Alive: The True Story of Usain Bolt*. New York, NY: Skyhorse Publishing, 2012.

Caioli, Luca. *Ronaldo: The Obsession for Perfection*. Crow's Nest, NSW, Australia: Corinthian Books, 2012.

Charyn, Jerome. *Joe DiMaggio: The Long Vigil*. New Haven, CT: Yale University Press, 2011.

Gay, Timothy M. *Satch, Dizzy & Rapid Robert: The Wild Saga of Interracial Baseball Before Jackie Robinson*. New York, NY: Simon & Schuster, 2010

Haney, Hank. *The Big Miss: My Years Coaching Tiger Woods*. New York, NY: Three Rivers Press, 2012.

Phelps, Michael, and Brian Cazeneuve. *Beneath the Surface: My Story*. New York, NY: Skyhorse Publishing, 2012.

Rice, Jerry, and Brian Curtis. *Go Long!: My Journey Beyond the Game and the Fame*. New York, NY: Ballantine Books, 2007.

Wahl, Grant. *The Beckham Experiment: How the World's Most Famous Athlete Tried to Conquer America*. New York, NY: Three Rivers Press, 2009.

Williams, Serena. *My Life: Queen of the Court*. New York, NY: Simon and Schuster, 2009.

INDEX